To the countless talented tradesmen

and women who have helped make

my dreams and visions a reality.

**andice Olson** is one of North America's leading designers and most recognized media personalities. As designer and host of *Divine Design with Candice Olson* and *Candice Tells All,* she is a favorite with viewers on W Network in Canada and HGTV in the U.S. Each week she brings a wealth of design experience and an attitude that is smart, witty, and truly unique into over 115 million North American households.

After earning her degree from the School of Interior Design at Ryerson University in Toronto, Candice launched an exciting commercial and residential design business. Considered "the one to watch" by *The New York Times,* Candice continued to receive accolades and media attention for her distinctive and exceptional work.

Candice's foray into television began when a local TV station profiled one of her award-winning design projects. Her unique approach to residential design and engaging personality led to a weekly stint as a design contributor to the show. Viewer demand for "more Candice!" led to the creation of the hit series, *Divine Design with Candice Olson.* Candice and the show quickly won a huge and loyal audience and went on to achieve a milestone of over 200 episodes after eight seasons. *Divine Design with Candice Olson* continues to receive rave reviews and recognition around the world, including the more than 160 countries where the series has aired.

In 2005, Candice launched the Candice Olson Collection, her own successful brand of licensed product lines, including upholstered furniture, fabrics, wallpaper, lighting, carpeting, case goods, and bedding. Candice's signature style is one she describes as "a fusion of traditional form, scale, and proportions, with the clean, crisp, simple beauty of modern design." For more information, visit www.candiceolson.com.

The continued demand for "more Candice!" brought her to wider audiences through guest appearances on television shows such as *The Today Show, Live! With Regis and Kelly, The View,* and *The Oprah Winfrey Show.* Candice writes a bi-weekly newspaper column syndicated in over 400 newspapers across North America and is a frequent contributor to design magazines both in Canada and the U.S. For two seasons, Candice has been featured as a Celebrity Judge for the prime-time hit reality show *HGTV Design Star.*

Candice spends her free time with her family, skiing in the winter and relaxing at the beach in the summer. A native of Calgary, Alberta, she lives in Toronto with her husband and two children.

Table of Contents

2 Dining Rooms

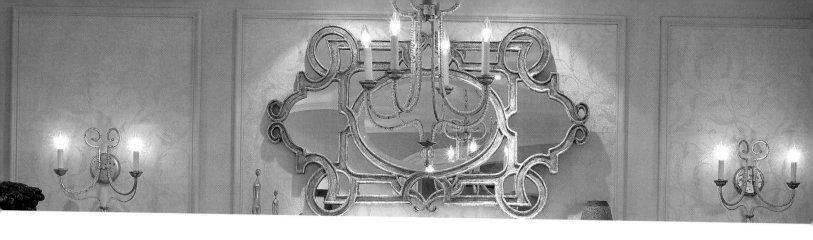

3

Living-Dining Combinations

4

Family Rooms and Great Rooms

5 Loft Living

A Place to Call Home   184

Custom built-ins and personal touches turn a small loft into a beautiful, multifunctional refuge for a young professional.

Lofty Ideas   192

Soaring ceilings and huge windows set the stage for a stylish transformation.

6

Basements (Yes, Basements!)

WANT TO KNOW WHERE CANDICE SHOPS?

As her fans around the world know, Candice Olson sources out the most amazing products from her favorite suppliers across North America, and now you can gain access too!

Visit **www.candiceolsonbooks.com** to find detailed information about the materials and products from all of her spectacular rooms in this book.

Happy shopping!

INTRODUCTION

Years ago, after a day of skiing with friends, we were invited to their new home for après-ski drinks and snacks. For years they had been looking for an all-season vacation property close to the ski hill, and they had recently found the perfect place: a charming, historical (real-estate-speak for condemned money pit/fixer-upper) farmhouse. They had just embarked on the first phase of what would prove to be endless renovations, so they told us to meet them back at the farmhouse in 15 minutes and to head for the pig barn. That's where they had set up a makeshift dining room for the holidays. Pig barn?! No matter how you said it, a date at "Swine and Dine" or "Chez Piggy" didn't really conjure up notions of elegance and style! Oh, how wrong I was . . . .

To set the record straight, the pigs had vacated the premises long ago, along with the previous owner. That said, the building was as rustic as rustic gets, with exposed-wood walls and beams, soaring rafters, and a roaring fire burning in the cast-iron stove in the corner.

All of this would play a role in setting the stage for a magical night.

Candle lanterns illuminated a wall of firewood stacked floor to ceiling. The play of light and shadow on the wood created an intimate, textured backdrop for a table made from a huge barn-board door surrounded by benches of hay bales covered in cozy wool blankets. A votive-candle chandelier adorned with sparkling bits of old costume jewelry hung from a wood beam above the table. More votives floated in a long feeding-trough-turned-ice-bucket and raked light up across wood plank walls—gorgeous!

Beside the cast-iron stove, a workbench displayed an assortment of casual snacks and hors d'oeuvres, all served in mix-and-match flea market china and crystal dishes, adding a whimsical and sparkling bit of posh to the nosh!

We ate, drank, and laughed into the wee hours, and when I left, I couldn't help but feel as if I had just left an upscale banquet hall, not a humble old barn.

The décor of this evening epitomized the essence of my philosophy of everyday elegance. The look was casual and carefree with an unexpected, somewhat cheeky wink at glamour and sophistication. The space had been selectively edited based on beauty or interest as well as purpose and function, so that what was left reflected a unified yet seemingly effortless grace and style.

There was also a comforting sense of quality and longevity that defied the temporary use of the space. This old barn had been around for a hundred years, and although it was weathered and worn, it felt as if it would be around for another century.

There were dramatic contrasts of rustic and refined, ornate and plain, and matte and lustrous, creating visual interest and perfectly capturing the character of our hosts. This space truly expressed their unique style: free-spirited, eclectic, and creative. That is exactly what you want your home's décor to do, even if you call a pig barn home!

Everyday elegance isn't a matter of expensive furnishings and high-end luxury materials. Rather, it's an attitude, a finesse that's expressed in the confident blending of colors, textures, and styles to create a setting that is timeless, comfortable, and entirely your own. Of course, a little sparkle and bling is always nice, which is exactly why the next time I'm invited to the Pig Barn I'll be sure to bring some of my mismatched earrings to add to the candle chandelier!

1

LIVING ROOMS

A ROOM WITH A VIEW

CHALLENGE

Wanda's swanky new condo on the thirty-fourth floor has big windows, beautiful hardwood floors, and an incredible view of Lake Ontario. But her ornate, overstuffed, and fringed furnishings feel too heavy and traditional for this clean, contemporary space. Wanda loves to entertain and wants this room to be not only a comfortable place for relaxing and watching TV but also a streamlined, stunning setting for conversation and cocktails. I have a plan for taking the space to new heights of sophistication!

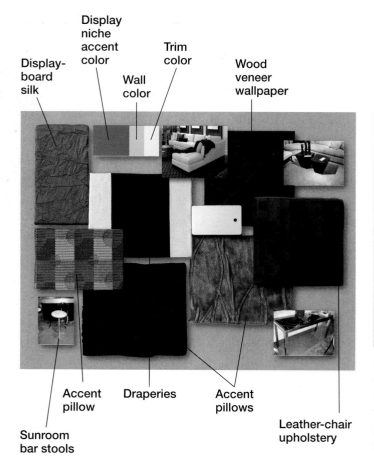

Display niche accent color

Display-board silk

Wall color

Trim color

Wood veneer wallpaper

Accent pillow

Draperies

Accent pillows

Sunroom bar stools

Leather-chair upholstery

BEFORE: Wanda's formal, traditional furniture and huge Oriental rug looked great in her old home, but in this new, modern condo they felt overbearing and out of place. The television had been purchased to fit a specific spot, but the niche below seemed to be waiting for a fireplace that would never come.

AFTER: New, clean-lined furniture and a dramatic "fireplace wall" treatment give the living room the sophisticated, modern look Wanda wants. Now the room is as spectacular as the view!

SOLUTION

- Wanda had bought a television to fit an existing niche in what looked like a fireplace elevation, but with 10-inch-thick concrete walls, there was no way to put in a fireplace. Instead, I built out the elevation with a display niche on each side and created a wood insert paneled with mirror to fit where a fireplace would ordinarily go.

- Bringing in the modern look required a complete rethinking of Wanda's furniture. Out went the big Oriental rug and all the heavy, traditional seating. In its place I brought in a large sectional with a chaise that can seat seven or eight people comfortably. Floating this piece in the center of the room defines a better traffic path to the windows and creates a much more welcoming look than furniture lined up against the walls.

- A pair of low-backed, armless slipper chairs are perfect in front of the big windows because they don't block the view. An upholstered armchair rounds out the conversation area.

- In the little alcove off the living room, I placed a bar table and chairs to create an intimate nook for cocktails and enjoying the view.

- The concrete ceiling meant that I couldn't install recessed lighting, but I moved the existing track lighting closer to the wall to make the low ceiling seem larger. Extending the track into the solarium nook let me drop a little pendant over the bar table.

ABOVE: A custom cabinet on wheels tucks into each niche to provide storage and display space and can be pulled out when necessary to uncover the air conditioning vent.

OPPOSITE: To downplay the television, I added a display niche on each side and covered the entire elevation in a stunning black wallpaper. A custom-designed mirrored insert under the TV creates the effect of a fireplace and makes a suitably elegant focal point for the room.

STYLE ELEMENTS

- The big black TV stuck out like a sore thumb against those white walls. To blend it into the setting and unify the whole "fireplace" elevation, I covered the entire area with an incredible wallpaper of ebony-stained wood veneer.

- The black wallpaper inspired a high-contrast, high-impact color scheme of red, black, and white. For dramatic punch, I painted the display niches on either side of the TV a rich, bold red.

- I toned down the white walls slightly with a coat of soft cream that flows around the entire space, including the doors, to keep the space from feeling chopped up.

- The color scheme continues at the windows, with graphic black-and-white-striped draperies that frame the magnificent view.

- To balance the TV wall, I hung large upholstered display boards on the opposite wall. They're covered in a fabulous crinkly red silk that shows off artwork matted in white and framed in black. To ensure that the fabric wouldn't lose its texture when it was stretched tightly over the boards, it was backed with fusible interfacing first.

RIGHT: A clean-lined, contemporary sectional and an iconic modern coffee table sweep away every trace of traditional in Wanda's new living room. The sectional's creamy Ultrasuede upholstery harmonizes with the walls and stands out against the red silk display boards. Picture lights over the boards add sparkle and supplement the track lighting, which I moved closer to the walls to make the ceiling seem more expansive.

ABOVE: Sleek, super-cool bar chairs and a contemporary bar table turn this sunny nook into an intimate little spot for cocktails.

LEFT: Brown leather slipper chairs and a graphic brown-and-tan area rug pick up on the warm, rich tone of the wood floors. Black-and-white-striped draperies frame the gorgeous view and help make the off-center windows look centered.

DESIGNED FOR MEDIA AND MORE

CHALLENGE

Chris and Alison are working their way through an entire top-to-bottom, back-to-the-studs renovation of a little Victorian townhouse, but it has turned out to be a monster of a job. They're doing all the work themselves, and they've gotten the second floor to an almost-livable point. On the first floor, they've torn out what had been two small bedrooms and a bathroom with the goal of making it their main living area, where they can watch TV, read, and entertain friends. The space has loads of potential, but they're drowning in crumbling plaster and have called on me to help rescue them from their renovation woes.

Love seat upholstery

Cabinetry

Stainless-steel fireplace surround

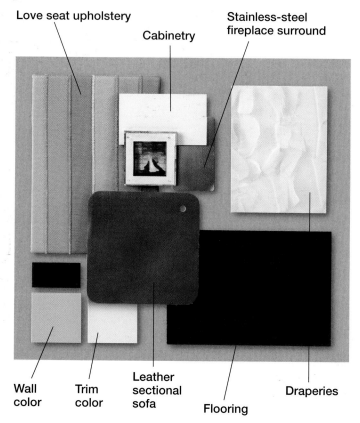

Wall color

Trim color

Leather sectional sofa

Flooring

Draperies

BEFORE: Welcome to renovation chaos! With walls torn out and plaster removed back to the lath in spots, the opened-up space was still a very long way from the relaxed and elegant living room Chris and Alison envisioned.

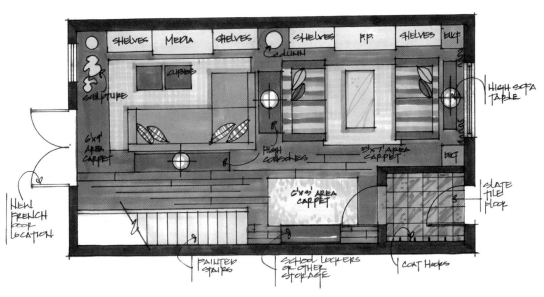

AFTER: Beautiful new cabinetry defines the character of the space and divides the room into zones for TV watching and reading, relaxing, and conversation. Furniture placement creates visual walls that carve out traffic paths and give each zone its own snug sense of enclosure while maintaining the open feeling.

SOLUTION

- The room had to be rebuilt from scratch, with new floors, walls, cabinetry, lighting, furniture—the works! I started by putting up drywall on the walls and ceiling and trimmed out the room with new baseboards, door frames, and window frames in traditional moldings with a corner block detail, in keeping with the age of the house.

- After ripping out the old flooring, I laid a new subfloor and topped it with prefinished hardwood flooring. I also painted the stairs to match the new flooring and installed simple spindles and a handrail.

- The entry had a side wall but nothing else, so I completed building out the foyer, laid a waterproof slate floor, and installed a mullioned reeded-glass door to let light in.

- To create better flow between the living room and dining room, I closed off a tiny doorway that had connected the two and created a new, larger opening with French doors (see the floor plan on page 27).

- To make the most of the long, skinny space, I divided it into two zones, one half for a library and the other half for a media zone. Custom-built wood cabinetry defines the two areas, and mirror backing on the bookshelves helps expand the sense of space—which helps compensate for the fact that the cabinetry made the room a little narrower! A gorgeous focal-point gas fireplace, installed at seated-eye level, anchors the library area, and the television is the obvious focal point for the media end of the room. With a mix of open and closed storage, the cabinetry is super-functional and really defines the character of the space.

OPPOSITE: Beautiful built-in cabinetry with traditional details adds architectural character to the renovated living room. In the "library zone," the gas fireplace anchors the cozy seating group, and mirror backing on the bookshelves visually expands the room by reflecting light and views.

RIGHT: At the TV end of the living room, bookshelves snugly wrap an L-shaped sectional, providing storage and display space and defining the traffic path through the room. Wide-plank prefinished flooring is durable and hardwearing but has the right look of age for the house. Recessed lighting around the perimeter of the room washes light down on the walls and cabinets, and a stainless-steel artichoke-style pendant adds a contemporary industrial feeling.

STYLE ELEMENTS

- To speak to the vintage character of the house, I designed the cabinetry with traditional crown molding and recessed-panel doors outlined with a simple filet molding.

- The flooring, a prefinished hardwood stained a very dark brown, has a raked finish that looks salvaged, like it has been there forever.

- Chris and Alison like retro and industrial style, so I balanced the traditional bones with more contemporary furnishings and even worked in some stainless-steel finishes.

- An olive-colored leather sectional offers super-comfy seating for watching TV, and a pair of smart, tailored love seats covered in a sage, olive, and camel stripe fits neatly into the area in front of the fireplace. The stripe adds color and graphic punch without calling too much attention to itself.

- The striped fabric suggested a quiet, nature-inspired color scheme of soft olive for the walls and creamy white for the cabinetry, trim, and stair balusters. Using a creamy hue rather than bright white lowers the contrast and helps make this narrow room feel larger.

- To bring in the industrial element, I chose a fireplace with a wide stainless-steel surround trimmed with corner bolts and installed a retro-style stainless-steel ceiling fan.

- Every space needs a little something unexpected. For this room it's the drapery fabric—a fun and funky silk with torn strips of silk sewn to the backing. It looks like feathers!

RIGHT: A beautiful silk fabric that resembles feathers softens the windows and adds a fun, unexpected texture to the room. Woven-wood blinds provide light control. A contemporary stainless-steel sculpture tweaks the room's traditional style with a nod to shiny industrial finishes.

ABOVE: Camel, beige, and striped pillows break up the expanse of olive green on the leather sectional and tie this end of the room to the library zone. I enlarged some of Alison's photographs and framed them in black frames with white mats. Hung in a column at the foot of the stairs, they have a huge impact and make a dramatic, personal statement.

RADICAL REINVENTION

CHALLENGE

Ava and Dave are embracing some pretty amazing changes in their lives: She's an IT consultant by day but has begun performing as a standup comedian by night. He just gave up a successful career in real estate to return to his roots in broadcasting—and he's exploring rap music as a hobby. They want the living room in their new home to be as exciting as the new directions they're taking, but with its 1960s minty-green walls, worn carpet, and big brick-and-stone fireplace, the room is way out of sync with their fun, funky, and creative personalities. I have something in mind that I call techno-licious!

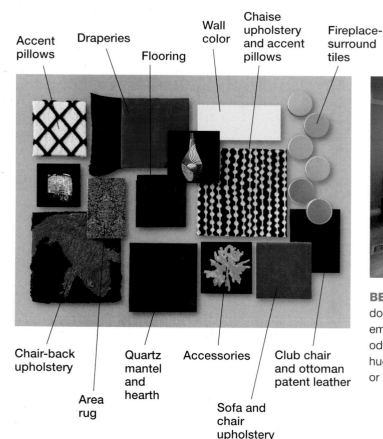

Accent pillows · Draperies · Flooring · Wall color · Chaise upholstery and accent pillows · Fireplace-surround tiles

Chair-back upholstery · Area rug · Quartz mantel and hearth · Accessories · Sofa and chair upholstery · Club chair and ottoman patent leather

BEFORE: Vivid walls and a massive brick-and-stone fireplace dominated the large living room, and acres of worn carpet emphasized the ho-hum, out-of-date feeling. The couple's odds and ends of furniture floated aimlessly in the space or hugged the walls, so the room wasn't particularly functional or welcoming.

AFTER: What's black and white and red all over? No, not a sunburned zebra! A fantabulous, high-tech-inspired transformation that combines high contrast with luscious, high-touch textures. Add a sprinkling of sparkle and you have a bold and sophisticated setting for relaxing and entertaining.

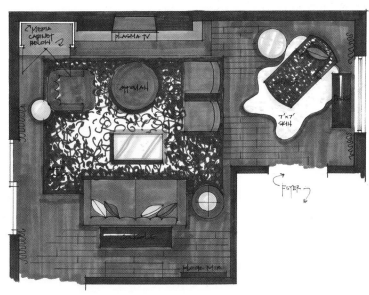

ABOVE: Now the fireplace dominates the room in a good way! The dramatic tile and quartz surfaces mask the old brick, and recessed lights set into the side of the fireplace call attention to the shimmery metallic paint treatment. Koi-patterned fabric gave the cue for the color scheme.

SOLUTION

- I started with the fireplace, which was the room's focal point—but not in a good way. Instead of tearing it out, I used the massive brick-and-stone structure as the base for a much more dramatic treatment: I built out the wall above it to hold a recessed flat-panel TV and then covered the existing hearth with one long, new hearth. A new continuous mantel stretches across the fireplace and into the corner, where it tops a new custom-built cabinet.

- After ripping up the carpet, I laid down a prefinished hardwood floor, one of the changes Ava and Dave specifically asked for.

- The room badly needed new lighting. I installed recessed lights in the ceiling around the entire perimeter of the room for overall illumination. For some "look at me" accents, I added over-the-top crystal sconces above the mantel and set miniature 20-watt recessed lights into the fireplace surround to shoot out light horizontally along the wall.

- I also installed a new sound system and speakers in the ceiling. Everything is remote-controlled, so Ava and Dave can change the mood with the touch of a button.

BELOW: I put this little corner to work with a sleek, dark-wood cabinet topped by an extension of the hefty quartz mantel. Media equipment is stored in here.

STYLE ELEMENTS

- The drama starts with the over-mantel and hearth, which I covered in a beautiful ebony quartz with a sparkly silver fleck.

- I picked up on the silver with large-scale penny tiles in a stainless-steel finish for the surround. About the size of silver dollars, the tiles have a retro Las Vegas vibe. They're made of terra-cotta with a stainless-steel cap and are attached to a mesh backing to make installation relatively easy. I used gray grout to blend them with the black quartz.

- I painted all of the walls bright white, then carried the silver element onto two walls with wide silver and pearl stripes. A steely gray basecoat gives a touch of color to the silver bands, which have a top coat of silver latex paint. A pearl glaze adds richness and subtle sparkle to the plain white bands.

- To ground all of the metallics, I chose dark-stained flooring with a smooth, tight grain. It has a modern look yet balances the cool metals with natural warmth.

- A frame-worthy fabric featuring red koi on a black background nods to Ava's Asian heritage and provided the perfect starting point for upholstery and drapery choices. Black patent leather for a club chair and ottoman, red velvet for the sofa and chairs, and a luminous red silk for the draperies play off the quartz and stainless steel. Lots of accent pillows in solids and prints splash color and pattern around the room and help soften the bold, high-contrast scheme.

LEFT: The new living room is all about techno-inspired metallic sparkle balanced by the touchable warm textures of matte velvet and dark wood. Covering the fireplace required us to attach cement board over the brick and apply an adhesive mortar mix so the quartz would have something to adhere to. The framed mirror disappears when the TV is turned on.

ABOVE: Clean, straight lines give the sofa, chairs, and coffee table a contemporary edge, which I like to balance with subtle traditional touches such as the button-tufted ottoman and the pedestal side table. Pillow fabrics pick up on the "fishy" koi theme with the look of fishnet and fish eggs.

LEFT: The only window in the living room is in an alcove between the foyer and the main living area. I framed it with shimmering silk draperies and turned the alcove into a mini-sanctuary for reading and relaxing with a comfy chaise upholstered in a subtle tone-on-tone gray stripe. The drapery fabric needs to be weighted to hang well, so I had a cotton-covered lead string stitched into the hem. It's unnoticeable yet makes the draperies fall beautifully.

BELOW: Wide silver and pearl stripes on this wall mirror the bands of color on the fireplace wall. With so much contemporary, graphic pattern elsewhere in the room, I chose a super-ornate, lace-patterned black-and-white rug to anchor the living area. It answers the cool, sophisticated elegance of the rest of the room with an unexpectedly baroque touch.

A WELL-FEATHERED NEST

CHALLENGE

Between maintaining a busy law practice and caring for her active two-year-old daughter, Sylvia hasn't had time to do much in the way of decorating the living room in her new home. It's the main living space in a charming older house, with leaded-glass bay windows, beautiful hardwood floors, and traditional trim work. This is where Sylvia spends time with her daughter, and what color there is comes from Chloe's toys. Sylvia would love for the room to be a comfortable, sophisticated place to relax with adult friends and still be child-friendly for Chloe.

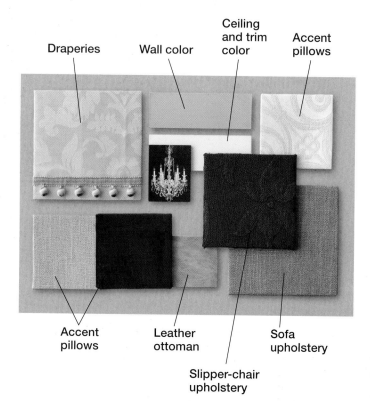

Draperies · Wall color · Ceiling and trim color · Accent pillows

Accent pillows · Leather ottoman · Slipper-chair upholstery · Sofa upholstery

BEFORE: With beautiful floors and handsome architecture, the living room had loads of potential but not much in the way of furniture. Sylvia didn't know whether the fireplace worked, and the curvy little wooden valance across the bay window didn't really go with the style of the house.

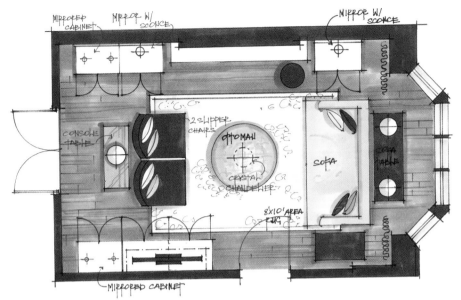

AFTER: Our legal-eagle's nest is now feathered to perfection! Adult-friendly seating in kid-proof fabrics welcomes Sylvia and daughter Chloe as well as friends. Thanks to a new gas insert, the fireplace is now a functioning focal point.

SOLUTION

- Making this room a space that works for mom-and-child play as well as adult conversation starts with storage. A store-bought storage system along two walls at one end of the room stashes toys, DVDs, and books out of sight and provides attractive display space for grownup collectibles. Mirror backing, glass shelves, and in-cabinet puck lights customized the ready-to-assemble units.

- After making sure the fireplace was properly vented, I installed a gas insert to solve the question of functionality. A coat of paint updates the mantel.

- With an old plaster ceiling, recessed lights weren't really an option, so instead I put up a track with spotlights above the TV (see pages 46 and 47).

- To make the room feel a little brighter and more spacious, I installed large custom mirrors on the cabinets flanking the fireplace. I designed them to fit with the store-bought cabinets, so the effect is seamless. Sconces mounted through the mirrors throw out twice as much sparkly light thanks to the reflection.

- New furniture organizes the room around the fireplace, with a three-seater sofa in front of the bay window, a pair of slipper chairs opposite, and a round ottoman (no sharp corners to hurt Chloe!) in the center. The slipper chairs can easily be reoriented to the television when it's just Sylvia and Chloe at home.

LEFT: A large mirror panel mounted on the wall beside the fireplace expands the apparent width of the room by reflecting light and the view of the space. Teal walls inspired by the fabric choices play up the architectural features.

ABOVE: A ready-to-assemble storage system lets you configure upper and lower cabinets with open and closed storage to best fit your needs. I customized the upper cabinets with glass shelves and in-cabinet lighting. Slipper chairs are a good choice for small rooms because they offer maximum seating surface in a minimum of space.

STYLE ELEMENTS

- This room needed to be kid friendly but elegant and feminine. The teal-and-gold-striped damask for the draperies is both elegant and girly and provided the jumping-off point for the room's color scheme.

- I chose a fantastic sofa covered in indestructible linen for the main seating. The design is named Tina because of its sexy legs and short skirt! For the slipper chairs, I selected a subtle tonal damask pattern in brown that has a velvety quality and speaks to the drapery fabric.

- Ottomans that double as coffee tables take a lot of wear and tear, so for a piece that's going to see a lot of stress, what could be better than distressed butterscotch leather? It will only get better looking with time.

- To play off the crisp white storage system, I painted the walls a teal color that matches the sofa upholstery and drapery fabric.

- Accent pieces in dark chocolate wood tones pick up the color of the brown velvet slipper chairs and add warmth and weight to the color scheme.

- For a gorgeous bit of bling, I hung a dazzling crystal chandelier perfectly centered in front of the fireplace and installed matching sconces on the two mirror panels. Nothing says feminine elegance like crystal!

BELOW: I gave the fireplace a fresh facelift with a coat of white paint. The butterscotch-leather ottoman is a super-functional piece, with storage below and comfy seating on top that can also serve as a coffee table. The warm color of the leather balances the cool teal of the walls, and a beautiful area rug in muted tones of caramel and steely blue pulls the whole room together.

OPPOSITE: With a flirty short skirt and curvy legs, this sofa design earns its name Tina (as in Turner). A gently shaped back and narrow arms give the piece a traditional look with a modern twist. The sofa sits in front of the bay but doesn't block the radiator that heats the room. I treated the entire bay as a single window with woven-wood blinds for light control and nonfunctioning draperies for elegant framing.

ABOVE: The clean, contemporary look of the modular storage system, with its flat-faced, flush-mounted doors and sleek bar handles, contrasts with the traditional style of the architecture. I like to combine contemporary and traditional styles this way to keep the look fresh and up-to-date. The simplicity of the cabinetry also suits small spaces because it doesn't distract the eye with details.

OPPOSITE: Placing the TV up on the cabinets keeps it out of Chloe's reach and at comfortable eye level for viewing. A track with spotlights on the wall above helps bring some overall lighting to this corner of the room.

START WITH THE ART

CHALLENGE

Fresh from a romantic wedding in the Caribbean, world travelers Nimi and Serge have come home to a new townhouse. In most of the house they've successfully combined their furnishings and art collections to reflect their eclectic tastes. The one room that's still crying out for attention is the second-floor family room. It's painted a boring neutral and has a small bay window and an enormously high ceiling—so high that even *I* feel overwhelmed by the space! They've asked me to make it a chic, contemporary living room and a showcase for their art—in time for a post-nuptial party.

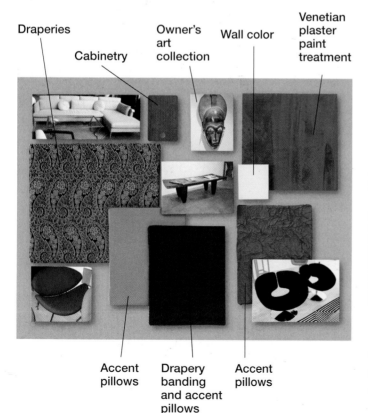

Draperies

Cabinetry

Owner's art collection

Wall color

Venetian plaster paint treatment

Accent pillows

Drapery banding and accent pillows

Accent pillows

BEFORE: A soaring ceiling, limited floor space, and a small bay window make furniture arrangement a real challenge in this second-floor living room. The slouchy, overscaled leather sofas and ready-to-assemble bookcase don't reflect the chic, contemporary, eclectic style the couple aspires to.

AFTER: Long, low, ebony-stained storage floats on the wall behind a new, streamlined sectional sofa. The sectional is great for lounging as well as seating a crowd, and I like the way it shapes the space. It's positioned to open toward the entrance to the room, so the effect is very welcoming.

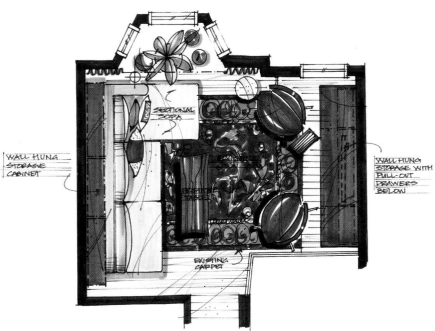

WALL HUNG STORAGE CABINET

SECTIONAL SOFA

WALL HUNG STORAGE WITH PULL-OUT DRAWERS BELOW

EXISTING CARPET

SOLUTION

- The soaring ceilings are both the biggest asset and the biggest challenge in this space. To bring the room down to a more human scale, I painted the lower part of the walls a deep royal blue and the walls above a light, neutral tone. To relate the band of color to the architecture, I aligned it with the stair landing.

- To provide much-needed storage and display space, I installed long, low cabinets on the two longest walls. On one side of the room, three cubbies provide open storage at floor level and hold the flat-screen TV at 30 inches above the floor, perfect for viewing from the seating across the room. On the opposite wall, floating open storage stretches along the entire length of the wall.

- I replaced the big leather sofas with one sleek, contemporary sectional that includes a chaise. It sits right in front of the wall-hung storage unit and opens toward the stairs, creating a welcoming, "come on in" feeling.

- One of the items Nimi and Serge particularly wanted me to include in the room was a massive chandelier Serge had found in a Mexican flea market. A handcrafted art piece that represents the universe, it had to be hoisted up and attached to a heavy chain—and it definitely supplies the "wow" factor this room needed!

- For additional drama, I installed a few accent lights in the tops of the storage units to send beams of light up the walls. Under-shelf lighting also highlights collections.

RIGHT: Shots of bold blue, red, and gold on the walls and accent pillows pull the colors of the carpet up into the room. I hung some of the couple's paintings on the walls and propped others so they can easily be rotated to show off more of the collection.

ABOVE: Dark wood cabinetry and a long, low, streamlined sectional anchor the soaring space and bring the focus down to a more human level. To balance those horizontals with some verticals, I framed the windows with draperies and used art, plants, and even the mirror to lift the eye.

ABOVE: The stair landing provided the logical guideline for the height of the Venetian plaster paint treatment and the new custom cabinetry. Fixtures installed in the top of the cabinetry shoot dramatic lighting up the wall, while under-shelf fixtures highlight the paint treatment showing through the open-back shelves. Low contemporary chairs don't block the view of the TV from the sectional.

STYLE ELEMENTS

- The other item Nimi and Serge wanted to keep in the room was Nimi's beautiful Oriental carpet. I used it as the jumping-off point for all of the colors in the space, from the royal blue paint treatment to the gorgeous, exotic silk draperies and blue, red, and gold accent pillows.

- To give added richness to the band of blue on the walls, I applied a Venetian plaster treatment. This time-consuming paint technique involves applying a dark blue basecoat followed by three coats of plaster, each coat tinted with a progressively lighter tone of royal blue. You often see this treatment applied in a random cross-hatching pattern to simulate old plaster walls, but I wanted a vertical application here for a more formal look, almost like wainscoting.

- I replaced the dark, industrial-looking carpeting on the stairs with a light, neutral sisal for a more modern feeling. Then I carried that light color onto the walls above the blue band, all the way up to the ceiling.

- For the custom cabinetry, I chose a deep chocolate-brown stain. Like the blue band of paint, the dark-stained cabinetry helps bring the vast space down to a more intimate scale.

- With the blue band anchoring the space, I took color vertically with dummy panels of a gorgeous gold and blue paisley silk framing the windows. The fabric itself is elegant and exotic, but the installation is clean and contemporary, with grommets threaded on an industrial-looking metal rod.

- To round out the seating, I brought in a couple of modern pedestal-base chairs that are like artworks themselves—icing on the wedding cake for Nimi and Serge!

RIGHT: Serge's fantastic flea-market find, a huge chandelier, hangs over the new seating area. A Mexican artist's interpretation of the universe, it looks spectacular from above on the stairs as well as from below.

METRO LUXURY

Nadia, a young lawyer, and her brother, Jordan, who is still in law school, occupy an early-1980s ground-floor condo. They inherited the too-fancy draperies and tired neutral carpeting from the previous owners and have been living with hand-me-down furnishings, but Nadia is more than ready to make the transition from student style to adult sophistication. She'd like this "everything" space to be a luxurious, high-end entertaining enclave where she and Jordan can have real sit-down dinners and lots of conversation with friends. They've pleaded their case for a complete makeover, and I'm finding for the plaintiff!

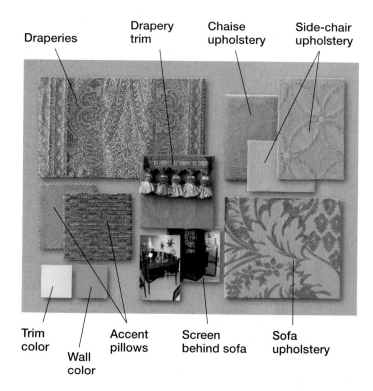

Draperies • Drapery trim • Chaise upholstery • Side-chair upholstery • Trim color • Wall color • Accent pillows • Screen behind sofa • Sofa upholstery

BEFORE: This style-starved, outdated condo suffered from bland beige carpeting, dated window treatments, and a random mix of old furniture. Only the chaise and coffee table reflected Nadia's effort to move from student days to adult style.

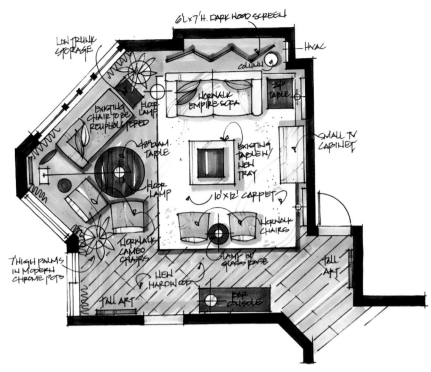

Floor plan labels:
- LOW TRUNK STORAGE
- 6'x7'H. DARK WOOD SCREEN
- HVAC
- COLUMN
- 34" TABLE
- EXISTING CHAIR TO BE REUPHOLSTERED
- FLOOR LAMP
- NORWALK EMPIRE SOFA
- 48" DIAM. TABLE
- EXISTING TABLE W/ NEW TRAY
- SMALL TV CABINET
- FLOOR LAMP
- 10'X12' CARPET
- NORWALK CHAIRS
- 7'HIGH PALMS IN MODERN CHROME POTS
- NORWALK CAMEO CHAIRS
- LAMP W/ GLASS BASE
- NEW HARDWOOD
- TALL ART
- TALL ART
- BAR CONSOLE

AFTER: The verdict is in: New flooring, elegant draperies, and sophisticated color on the walls take this space from desperately dull to dignified and dramatic. Traditional-style furniture that's in scale with the room organizes the space for function and versatility.

SOLUTION

- First I pulled up the old builder's-beige wall-to-wall carpeting and replaced it with thin-plank hardwood flooring. (Thin planks were important here, to allow enough clearance for the doors to open and close easily over them.) Because the planks couldn't be attached directly to the concrete floors, I first laid down a cork substrate, which helps control moisture and provides a surface to which the flooring can be glued.

- The awkwardly angled windows dominated the room and made furniture arrangement tricky, so I decided to lay the flooring on the diagonal, parallel to the two main windows. This makes sense of the angles and has the added advantage of appearing to stretch the dimensions of the space. As I always say, if you can't beat 'em, join 'em!

- I then designated the area near the windows as the dining zone. The remaining space became the new conversation/TV zone. I centered a new armoire for the TV on the back wall and flanked it with large framed mirrors to enlarge the sense of space. The mirrors hang on cleats that hold them about 1 inch from wall, so they appear to be floating.

- The room had only one lonely light fixture, but because the ceiling is stucco over concrete, I couldn't add junction boxes for more lights. My solution? I pulled the power from the existing ceiling box to an L-shaped track and installed spotlights that sculpt the space with light. For sparkly accent lighting, I installed sconces through the wall mirrors.

LEFT: A floor lamp stands in for a chandelier to illuminate the little dining area. I upholstered the small Louis XVI-style chairs in a mix of solids and geometrics to tweak the traditional style with a contemporary edge.

STYLE ELEMENTS

- To give this room the upscale, urban look Nadia wanted, I chose a sophisticated color scheme of grayed celadon green and champagne, with dark woods to give it weight.

- For the wood flooring, I selected a medium-tone pecan finish. The wood has a beautiful grain, and the red undertones complement the gray-green wall color.

- Sheer vertical blinds are the perfect solution for light control and privacy at the big windows. The sheers filter light during the day, and with a twist of the wand, the blinds enclosed between the fabric layers close to block light and views entirely.

- Pleated dummy panels in a very subtle paisley stripe frame each quirky window with luxury. They're banded in green silk to pick up the wall color and edged with tassels for a dressy touch. Instead of hanging them on drapery rods, I attached them with Velcro to wood strips just below the ceiling. This lets them hang in long columns from the ceiling to the floor, framing an uninterrupted expanse of filmy sheers. It's so gorgeous, it's criminal!

- Nadia's new chaise was a little too bulky and overscaled for the space, so I had it rebuilt for a cleaner, more style-savvy look. With new cream-colored mohair upholstery and a dark paint treatment for the wood frame and legs, it's now a timeless and sophisticated piece worthy of a rising young attorney.

- I placed the chaise parallel to the main window to anchor the dining zone and double as guest seating for big parties. A new 48-inch-diameter pedestal table in an ebony stain and a pair of side chairs complete this zone. Since I couldn't install a chandelier, I did the next best thing and brought in a swooping floor lamp with a pleated shade.

- Nadia's other purchase, a whitewashed French-style coffee table, inspired my seating choices for the conversation area: a curvy sofa covered in two-tone cut chenille damask and a pair of Louis XV-style open-arm chairs covered in a mix of geometrics for a contemporary look. The chairs can transition from the living area to the dining area as needed.

- To blend the coffee table into the new color scheme, I painted over the whitewashed finish with gold paint, then glazed it with ebony. With this elegant new look, the old glass top needed a little visual weight and interest, so I backed it with mirror and sandwiched a print of an orchid between the mirror and the glass. Just the thing!

ABOVE: New chairs in the Louis XV style have thick upholstered seats and padded backs for modern comfort. Like the dining chairs, they're covered in a mix of solids and geometrics for a contemporary twist. A mirror-topped brass side table is visually lightweight and clean-lined, playing off the darker wood and curvy lines of the chair.

ABOVE: Backing the curvy sofa with a contemporary, see-through folding screen adds height and an illusion of greater depth to the room. In addition to painting the coffee table, I turned the top into a feature by layering a print of an orchid between the glass top and a new mirror insert.

DINING ROOMS

FAMILY MATTERS

CHALLENGE

Cristina comes from a big Italian family, and her mother, three sisters, and their families show up regularly, laden with food for weekly feasts. Cristina and Gavin just moved to a sprawling 1960s home with a terrific large dining room, complete with big windows and a beautiful view. The problem is that their only furniture is a table that might seat six (in a pinch) and a few chairs. There's no place to set out food and no storage for dinnerware. Cristina would love to have an elegant, formal, but not-too-stuffy dining room that can handle a crowd—and I have just the recipe!

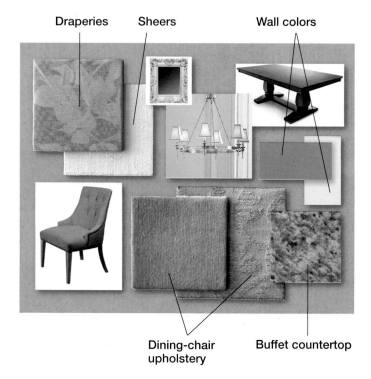

Draperies Sheers Wall colors

Dining-chair upholstery Buffet countertop

BEFORE: This big dining room was long on space and short on style and function. The dining table and chairs were not only lost in the room, they were completely inadequate for the huge family meals that Cristina and Gavin regularly host.

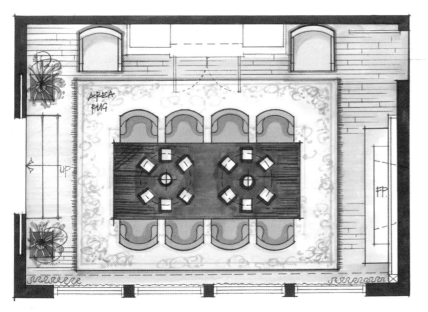

AFTER: A 10-foot-long table surrounded by super-comfy upholstered chairs guarantees a spot for everyone. New custom-built cabinetry provides serving space and storage, and I gave the dinky fireplace a major style boost to make it a real focal point in the large room.

SOLUTION

- Giving this room the heart-of-the-home look it needed starts with the fireplace—after all, what better symbol of family, food, hearth, and home? I covered the painted brick wall with drywall and replaced the outdated and too-small fireplace with a new gas insert. It features realistic-looking logs that are individually stacked—and pre-burnt!

- Then I installed a gorgeous cast-stone mantel and surround in a French limestone finish. It's both classic and contemporary and anchors the new look perfectly.

- To solve the storage and food service problem, I designed new cabinetry with lots of open and closed storage space for china, crystal, and linens. A long, continuous granite countertop makes a heat-resistant sideboard, allowing Cristina and Gavin to place hot casserole dishes directly on the surface for serving.

- This super-sized family needs a super-sized table, and I found just the thing: an 8-foot-long pedestal table with 2-foot extensions that can accommodate 10 people easily.

- The length of the table requires not one but *two* chandeliers. I added ceiling medallions to give the fixtures more presence and to add architectural interest to the big ceiling. I also updated the lighting with recessed ceiling fixtures and sconces above the fireplace.

RIGHT: A beautiful cast-stone surround and hearth look like hand-carved limestone and set the tone of old-world elegance and formal style that Cristina and her family wanted. The hearth is also roomy enough to perch on for after-dinner conversations— and maybe for roasting some marshmallows?

ABOVE: A custom-built buffet answers the need for storage and serving space. Mirror backing across the entire top section reflects light and the beautiful view of the woods beyond the windows on the opposite wall. In-cabinet lighting brings out the sparkle of crystal and bounces off the mirror backing to add to the sense of space and light.

STYLE ELEMENTS

- I designed the cabinetry to reflect the traditional look Cristina likes, but with country-style details to please Gavin's more rustic tastes. Recessed-panel doors and drawers have a simple cove reveal around the edge, and I chose bin-style pulls for the drawers. Crisp white paint, crown molding, and mirror backing give the whole piece a fresh, glamorous feel.

- My jumping-off point for the color scheme was an incredibly beautiful (and expensive) shimmery platinum drapery fabric that looks like leaves. I used it only for dummy panels to frame the windows, so even though it was pricey, I didn't need a lot of it to make a big impact on the room.

- To control light and help absorb noise, I also hung soft sheers that pick up on the silvery element in the platinum dummy panels. The fabric has a rippled, bark-like texture that speaks to the wooded view outside.

- The dining chairs are such a big feature in the dining room that I always try to give them as much visual interest as I can. I chose a streamlined barrel-back design that's deep and comfy for long dinner conversations and upholstered the chairs in a mix of fabrics—solid velvet chenille in soft aqua for the button-tufted fronts and a chenille filigree in taupe and aqua for the backs. Nailhead detailing picks up on the silvery metal finishes elsewhere in the room.

- When I pick wall colors, I always think about what will be sitting in front of the wall. For this room, I chose a creamy hue for the window wall and end walls to play up the drapery fabric and harmonize with the fireplace. For the wall behind the buffet, I chose a deep, smoky blue to emphasize the crisp white cabinetry and speak to the color of the dummy panels on the opposite wall.

OPPOSITE: Chrome chandeliers marry sleek modern style with a touch of tradition. The chrome finish speaks to the platinum hue of the dummy panels framing the windows and picks up on chrome details in the buffet hardware and on the sconces above the fireplace.

ABOVE: When this family gets together, there's a lot of talking and laughter, and it all echoes loudly in this big room. To absorb noise, I brought in fabrics at the windows and on the chairs. The carpet under the table not only helps with sound control, but also has a stain-hiding pattern that unifies the entire room. The serene blue-and-cream scheme here links up visually with the crisp white color scheme in the kitchen beyond.

BACK IN THE GAME

CHALLENGE

Ruhini and Barry embarked on a major renovation that originally included both the kitchen and the dining room. Unfortunately, after finishing their dream kitchen and installing new floors, baseboards, and crown molding in the dining room, they ran out of steam. Their two boys took over the space for indoor hockey games and a place to dump all their hockey gear, and when Ruhini and Barry entertain, they have to pull out a cafeteria-style table and folding chairs. The couple would like to reclaim the space and turn it into a real dining room, with a wood table and chairs that don't fold!

Dining-chair upholstery

Draperies   Drapery banding   Wallpaper   Fireplace wall color

BEFORE: Although the dining room had beautiful floors, baseboards, and crown molding, Barry and Ruhini had no dining room furniture, so there was plenty of space for the boys' piano and hockey gear. Oh, wait, this was supposed to be a *dining* room!

AFTER: Now *this* is a dining room! A new raised fireplace and rich, chocolate-brown grass cloth wallpaper create a warm and elegant setting for sit-down dinners and parties. A traditional, symmetrical layout organizes the space and puts the focus on the table—just what you would expect in a real dining room.

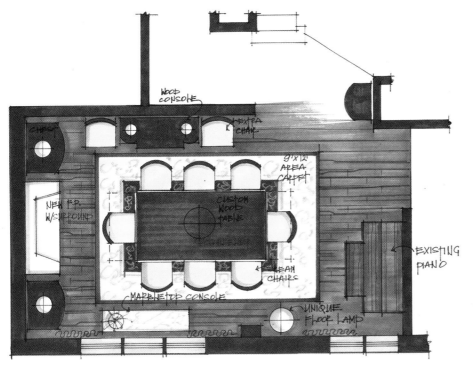

SOLUTION

- The dining room is visible from the entry, kitchen, and living room, so it needs to be special. My no-fail solution is to create a show-stopping focal point with a raised fireplace that you can see from outside the room and while seated at the table. I couldn't pull in a gas line, so I installed an electric fireplace instead.

- The painted-wood blinds at the windows were functional and in good condition, so I kept them and softened the walls with dummy panels that frame the openings.

- To solve the furniture problem, I brought in a 7-foot-long table that can extend to 10 feet when the leaves are added—plenty of room for big parties and company! The table anchors everything else in the room, so it has to have a huge "wow" factor. I went shopping at a mix-and-match warehouse to find the perfect top and a pedestal base, which lets you seat more people without bumping into the table legs.

- A dining table needs a chandelier, and a big table needs a big chandelier. I had to put in a new junction box in order to center the chandelier over the table instead of in front of the windows. Note to self: Junction boxes can't be plastered over because the electrical code says so. I discreetly disguised the old junction box with a plain white (removable) disk. The chandelier is so gorgeous that no one will notice it.

LEFT: A big six-arm chandelier matches the scale of the table and makes a major style statement: It's gorgeous, curvy, and elegantly traditional. Without the extensions, the table seats eight. Add the extensions, and Barry and Ruhini can seat even more.

ABOVE: Crisp white paint and traditional-style moldings link the new fireplace installation to the room's trim work and make it seem like it's always been there. Mirrored niches on either side of the fireplace double the apparent size of the room and help balance the rich, dark walls with reflected light.

STYLE ELEMENTS

- To create a spot for the fireplace, I built out the wall to contain the unit, then added architectural character with traditional crown moldings and pilasters built from medium-density fiberboard (MDF). This material is lighter than solid wood, is easy to install, and accepts paint beautifully. Under a smooth coat of crisp white, it looks just like wood.

- Since the room connects visually to the kitchen, I used the espresso finish of the kitchen island to guide my choices for the dining room. Grass-cloth wallpaper printed with a large-scale traditional damask pattern in tone-on-tone chocolate brown creates a rich, warm feeling, like wrapping the whole room in a big fuzzy sweater.

- The dark walls absorb a lot of light, so I chose the perfect six-arm chandelier to bring light back in. Its large scale suits the table, and its antique gold- and silver-leaf finish brings in an old-world, been-here-forever look that helps keep the space feeling casual and livable.

- Mirrors in the niches flanking the fireplace also help bring light into the room. Instead of big sheets of mirror, which would have been too contemporary for this space, I attached mirrored squares to the wall and affixed decorative rosettes over the meeting points. They give the treatment a hand-crafted look that reinforces the traditional style.

- To play off the dark walls, I chose a crisp cream linen for the drapery panels and banded the panels with chocolate velvet. Then I took it one wonderful step further and had the bands custom-embroidered with a design based on the wallpaper. This is a truly high-tech trick, by the way: The wallpaper design was scanned and fed into a laptop computer, which told the sewing machine exactly what to do, and it just stitched away!

- I had the table custom-stained a dark espresso color to echo the kitchen island. For the dining chairs, I chose a traditional style in the same wood tones as the table and upholstered the fronts and seats in cream and the backs in a small-scale print that picks up on the brown tones.

- For storage and display, I tucked a pair of chests into the niches beside the fireplace. Table lamps add to the ambient light, which the mirrors reflect back into the room to balance the dark walls.

OPPOSITE: Barry and Ruhini wanted the piano to stay in the room to remind the boys to practice. It will also be quite handy if they want some dinner music! A dummy panel hangs on just one side of the corner window, which helps unify it with the larger set of windows.

RIGHT: Custom-embroidered chocolate velvet banding adds a special touch to cream linen drapery panels. A painted table under the window provides display and serving space and balances a sideboard on the opposite wall.

3 LIVING-DINING COMBINATIONS

DAYCARE DÉCOR NO MORE

CHALLENGE

When Kelly and Dave moved from their downtown condo to a new home in the suburbs, they didn't have any furniture for the living room, so they turned it into a play space for their two toddlers. Soon it was so full of pup tents, playhouses, and toys that their neighbors thought the couple ran a daycare center! Now that the kids have lost interest in most of the toys, Kelly and Dave want to reclaim the living room for adults and make it, along with the dining room, the showpiece of the house—casual and comfortable, but also sparkly and elegant.

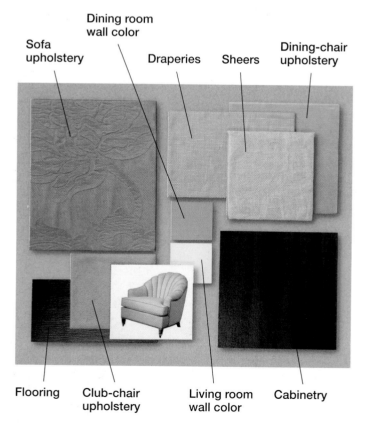

Sofa upholstery · Dining room wall color · Draperies · Sheers · Dining-chair upholstery · Flooring · Club-chair upholstery · Living room wall color · Cabinetry

BEFORE: No wonder visitors thought Kelly and Dave ran a daycare! Dave blocked off the opening between the living room and dining room with a low partition just to help contain the kid clutter.

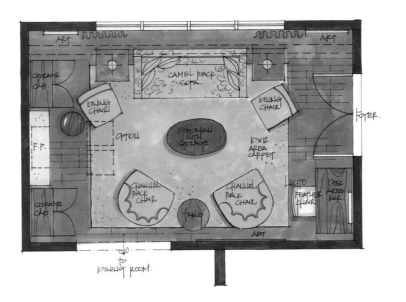
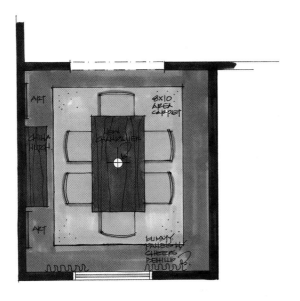

AFTER: Bye-bye, toy trains and plastic cars; hello, luscious elegance and grownup style! A beautiful new fireplace flanked by cabinetry creates a stunning focal point for the room. Furniture from my collection combines traditional references with clean, contemporary lines and is the perfect scale for a modern suburban living room.

ABOVE: New flooring updates the room and sits in contrast to the warm, creamy walls. An area rug helps define the conversation area and pulls the color scheme together. The living room is now toy-free, but I brought the toddlers back in by way of a big grouping of family photos on the wall. A paper template makes hanging an arrangement like this super-easy.

SOLUTION

- Every room needs a focal point, and the living room didn't have one. I remedied that situation right away with a fireplace front and center, flanked by storage cabinets. Because there hadn't been a fireplace here before, I chose an electric model—it's super-easy to install and doesn't need a flue, chimney, or gas line.

- Dave really wanted a TV in this room, but Kelly wasn't so thrilled with the idea. I found the coolest solution: a picture frame system that can be incorporated into the cabinetry. The flat-panel TV sits behind the picture frame, and when Kelly wants the TV to disappear, she simply presses a button on the remote control. A painting slides down over the television, completely concealing it.

- I pulled up the wall-to-wall carpeting and laid new, prefinished flooring over the existing, worn hardwood floor. Brazilian cherry plank flooring has a tight grain that's modern and sophisticated, just the look Kelly and Dave wanted.

- Since they had no living room furniture, I started from scratch to create a comfortable, cozy space for entertaining or just relaxing and watching TV. A couple of club chairs, a sofa, and a leather ottoman define an adult-friendly conversation area, and new upholstered chairs from the dining room can move into the living room if Kelly and Dave are hosting a crowd.

RIGHT: I tucked a small home-office area into the corner just inside the door, giving this room a little extra function. The desk chair can be moved over to the conversation area if there's a crowd. A beveled-edge mirror reflects more light and sparkle for Kelly.

STYLE ELEMENTS

- Kelly loves bling and shiny things, so I designed the focal-point wall with that in mind. The cabinetry doors are clad with triangular sections of mirror set in squares and punctuated with decorative rosettes. The edges of the mirrors catch the light and refract it, creating plenty of sparkle.

- Along with recessed lights in the ceiling for overall lighting, I brought in more sparkle with a small crystal pendant over the coffee table. It hangs lower than you would usually expect a fixture to hang, so it really catches attention. A modern crystal chandelier in the dining room adds more bling, sparkle, and shine!

- To create a casual yet elegant look, I chose furniture that combines contemporary, pared-down lines with traditional references. Channel-back club chairs on little wheeled feet recall their comfy Edwardian forebears, and a delicious camelback sofa with gently scrolled arms updates a timeless 18th-century design. I covered the club chairs with gold cotton velvet, and for the sofa, I chose an absolutely gorgeous metallic blue and gold stylized damask—bee-yoo-ti-full!

- The old sheers covering the wall of windows were overwhelming yet didn't do anything for the space. I replaced them with subtly embossed organza sheers to frame the sofa and softly diffuse the light. Gold dummy panels pick up on the damask and layer over the sheers, so the whole elevation ties together.

- To show off all of the shiny finishes, I chose a chocolate stain for the flooring and mahogany for the cabinetry.

- I warmed up the walls in the living room with a soft, creamy color and gave the dining room a little more drama with a smoky blue paint that pulls the blue of the damask into the next room.

RIGHT: Luscious gold dummy panels and an embossed organza frame the new camelback sofa and pick up on the shiny damask upholstery.

BELOW: A unique picture frame system above the fireplace allows the TV to disappear behind a painting at the touch of a button. The cast-stone fireplace surround anchors the focal-point wall in traditional style, while the coffee table introduces clean, modern lines. The seating pieces blend a little of each—familiar shapes and details with a contemporary twist. I like to accent conversation areas with unexpected lighting, like the crystal pendant over the coffee table.

OPPOSITE: Smoky-blue walls bring drama and intimacy to the dining room. Dark-chocolate wood finishes for the table and buffet relate to the living-room cabinetry to help tie the two spaces together visually. The crystal chandelier and beveled-edge mirror add more of Kelly's beloved bling!

RIGHT: Button-tufted dining chairs upholstered in creamy microfiber can move into the living room if needed. The window treatment matches the one in the living room to emphasize continuity between the two rooms.

THE ART OF CONVERSATION

CHALLENGE

Zoe and Lorne are a bundle of contradictions: Hip, young, and urban, they nevertheless love everything to do with Europe, including traditional old-world style and the old-fashioned art of conversation. They've just bought a 1940s house, and they are delighted with the windows, light, and layout. However, they're not so crazy about its bright pink walls. On top of that, their hand-me-down furniture, now about 25 years old, is ready for retirement. The couple already has a family room for TV watching, so they'd like this room to be all about European sophistication, conversation, and maybe a little music.

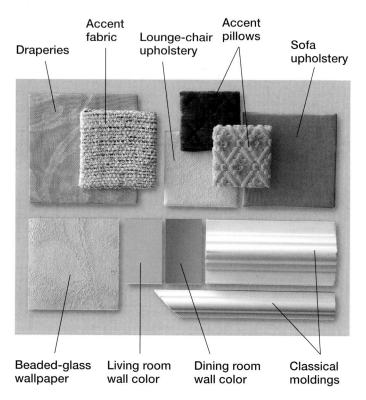

BEFORE: This 1940s house had nice moldings, a handsome fireplace, and beautiful hardwood floors, but the candy-pink walls in the living room gave Zoe and Lorne visual indigestion. They tried to make the best of it with their old hand-me-down gray sectional, but what they really wanted was some old-world elegance.

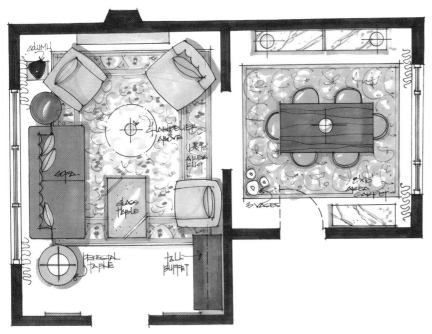

AFTER: Building on the existing architectural detail, I injected more traditional character with panel moldings on the wall and classic trim around the arch. New furniture captures a European sensibility without being too stuffy or formal. The dining room got a makeover to match, playing off the colors and textures in the living room.

SOLUTION

- The living room already had deep baseboards, crown molding, and a fireplace surround that spoke to traditional style. I built on that foundation with a simple, classic molding around the arch and added architectural character to the ceilings in this room and the dining room with medallions. I divided the fireplace wall into panels with a simple molding as well. Moldings are character-builders that instantly reference traditional European style, and these were economical and super-easy to install. They're made from lightweight Styrofoam coated with plaster and can be cut by hand with a miter box. They attach to the wall or ceiling with drywall compound.

- There wasn't a single light fixture in the living room, so before I got to any of the fun stuff, I had to run wiring through the ceiling and walls. Then I could install recessed ceiling lights, a gorgeous statement-making chandelier, and sconces, as well as some super-cool speakers for the new sound system.

- Furniture is a big part of creating European elegance and traditional flavor. The key piece for the living room is my Piper sofa, an overscaled model with traditional detailing, a high back, and a deep seat, perfect for the space. A modern take on a wing chair and a couple of low-arm side chairs fill out the conversational zone.

- Zoe and Lorne didn't really want technology to intrude on this space, so I brought in a beautiful French-inspired hutch. It looks nothing like a media cabinet but can double as media storage and a bar (see page 90). The 4-inch-deep speakers hang on the adjacent wall, concealed by photos printed on sound-permeable fabric. Framed in espresso-toned frames, they look like art!

- In the dining room, I kept the couple's existing dining table and updated the room with new upholstered chairs, a long sideboard for wine and cheese, and the big brother of the living room chandelier (see page 92).

- For the feature wall in the dining room, I created a focal point above the sideboard with a wall of mirrors (see page 93). Nine framed mirrors of varying sizes had to be fit together like a puzzle, so I laid them out on the floor first to figure out the arrangement before committing to nails in the wall.

RIGHT: The curvy lines of the beaded sconces and matching chandelier pick up on the swirly, stylized-leaf design of the beaded-glass wallcovering. Using this amazing material as an accent ups the "wow" factor without breaking the budget.

ABOVE: Zoe and Lorne wanted old-world elegance but with a sense of fun, so I combined traditional panel moldings and spectacular beaded-glass wallpaper insets with furniture and accessories that tweak traditional style. The super-scrolly mirror offers a playful take on rococo style, and the corner chair, with its rolled sides, updates the classic wing chair. I installed the panel moldings 6 inches in from the wall and floor and 4 inches from the ceiling so the center panel would align perfectly with the fireplace.

ABOVE: With dramatic oversize seating pieces and sumptuous, sparkly drapery panels, this has to be the most luxurious living room on this side of the pond! Matte-finish upholstery on the side chairs and a leather ottoman balance the sheen of the velvets and silks.

STYLE ELEMENTS

- Luscious velvety fabrics create the elegant atmosphere of a European-style salon. For the Piper sofa, I chose a celadon upholstery with a sheen that plays up the sculpted effect of the tufted back. Rich velvet accent fabrics, some with a washed treatment that makes them look aged, add to the old-world look.

- I planned to position the sofa in front of the windows, so the drapery fabric had to relate to the sofa upholstery. I found a stunning soft blue silk with a silvery stylized-leaf pattern. It was also pretty pricey, so I ordered just enough for dummy panels—the effect of draperies at a fraction of the cost! Soft, tactile sheers hang across the windows to diffuse light. They extend beyond the edge of the dummy panels by about 6 inches, so you'd never know the panels aren't fully functional.

- The drapery fabric gave me the key for wall colors. A light celery for the living room matches the tone of the stylized-leaf pattern. A rich teal accent fabric, a deeper tone of the blue, inspired a teal wall color for the dining room.

- I always like to include something unexpected in my designs, and in this living room, it was a spectacular beaded wallpaper set into the new wall panels. This wallcovering is an investment, but using it as an accent minimizes the cost and maximizes the spectacular, glam feeling.

- Lighting pulls together the European look. A beaded four-arm fixture in the living room speaks to the six-arm fixture in the dining room and to the matching sconces on the fireplace wall.

- For both rooms, I chose area rugs to anchor the seating. Rugs with an allover pattern don't dictate a particular furniture arrangement, so you have more flexibility for asymmetrical groupings.

LEFT: Lightweight plaster-coated Styrofoam moldings bring sophisticated, traditional style to the ceilings but are way easier to install than the 18th-century plaster moldings they're based on. I positioned recessed ceiling lights to highlight the beautiful luster of the drapery fabric.

OPPOSITE: A French-inspired hutch is actually a bar and media cabinet. The ebony finish adds weight to the room's light, shimmery color scheme and speaks to wood accents in the adjoining dining room.

ABOVE: What looks like a framed photo is actually a speaker for the sound system! The speaker is encased inside the 4-inch-deep frame and is covered by sound-permeable fabric. You can have your own photos printed on the fabric or use a stock photo.

RIGHT: The wall color of the living room appears on the ceiling of the dining room, tying the two rooms together. Moldings, lighting, and the window treatment also create visual links to unify the rooms.

OPPOSITE: With deep teal on the walls and new moldings and color on the ceiling, the dining room now has a more intimate, elegant feel in keeping with the living room. I kept the couple's table and updated it with new upholstered chairs, a new sideboard, and a wall of mirrors.

COMMAND PERFORMANCE

CHALLENGE

Doug and Cerrene have built their dream home, a spacious, light-filled place with lots of lovely traditional details. Right now, the living room and dining room are under-furnished and undecorated, but the couple envisions these two rooms as special-occasion spaces. They have one very unusual requirement: The design needs to work around a big, gold grand piano that Doug inherited from his father, who owned a popular restaurant where this piano was played nightly. Doug and Cerrene's two daughters are learning to play, so I'm going to give them a dramatic and glamorous setting that will really get their musical juices flowing.

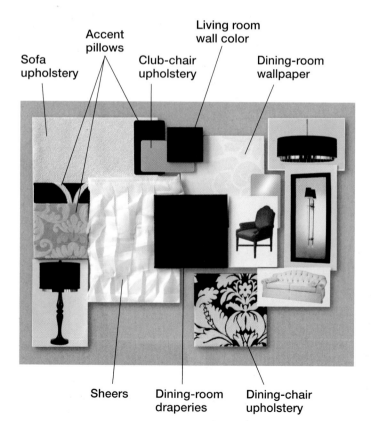

Sofa upholstery · Accent pillows · Club-chair upholstery · Living room wall color · Dining-room wallpaper · Sheers · Dining-room draperies · Dining-chair upholstery

BEFORE: This new home had lovely bones, but few furnishings and no drama—except for the gold piano! A small breakfast table stood in for dining room furniture.

AFTER: I tapped into my inner nightclub diva and came up with a black-tie design that puts the focus on performance. Dramatic black walls in the living room are balanced by crisp white in the dining room. I unified the two spaces by playing on the theme of black and white, with red and gold for accents.

SOLUTION

- First I needed to move the piano. Repositioning it in the corner beside the dining room put it right in the line of sight from the front door and freed up space for a long, beautiful sofa on one wall.

- Doug loved his sound system, but the 6-foot-tall speaker towers dominated the room—overwhelmed it, in fact. I replaced them with high-end bookshelf speakers that are just as powerful but much smaller. Doug can operate the sound system with an infrared remote control.

- I updated all of the furnishings in both rooms to create a more formal feeling and brought a pair of tall bookcases into the living room to flank the sofa. The bookcases add needed storage space and give a feeling of depth to the walls. In the dining room, I retired Cerrene's old table and brought in a larger one that seats 12 to 14 and better suits the size of the room.

- The dining room also needed storage and serving space. I designed a special feature: a floating sideboard with counter space for setting out a buffet (see page 98). Closed storage stretches to the ceiling to keep china, glassware, and serving pieces handy.

LEFT: Feathery sheers frame the windows in a long column that falls from the crown molding to the floor. The channel-back chairs have a little bit of an Edwardian-era feel that contrasts nicely with a modern mirrored chest.

ABOVE: Painting walls black can be tricky—you have to roll it all in one go, wet into wet, or else you'll get a patchy effect. Tall black bookcases blend into the wall yet add a subtle sense of depth with their gray backs. The seating pieces are formal and traditional, but the look is fresh and fun thanks to modern graphic accents—the pillows, clear acrylic coffee table, and cool contemporary wall art that relates directly to the piano.

STYLE ELEMENTS

- The piano establishes the function of the living room as piano room. Because it was gold, the challenge was how to blend it into the setting so it made sense. With the idea of black-tie performance in mind, I painted the walls black with a cool, bluish undertone. The black balances the warm gold of the piano and sets it off like a jewel in a black velvet box.

- To sit in front of that black wall, I chose a traditional camelback sofa with a tufted back, upholstered in crisp, clean white. At the end of the room, in front of the windows, I placed a pair of big, beautiful, luxurious channel-back club chairs upholstered in gold to balance the piano. Pillows in classic gold silk damask and modern black-and-white geometrics accent the solid upholstery.

- I dressed the windows in both rooms in a fun, feathery sheer that looks a lot like a flapper dress from the 1920s.

- The dining room had no style to speak of, and Cerrene and Doug envisioned something traditional but lighthearted. I reversed the black-and-white scheme from the living room and did a white-and-black scheme here, starting with a soft white, large-scale damask wallpaper for a little formality.

- Dining chairs with a scrolled crest continue the traditional theme, as does the upholstery, a graphic black-and-white damask that picks up on the pattern of the wallpaper.

- To contrast with the chairs and wallpaper and bring in a clean, contemporary element, I designed super-functional custom black cabinetry. The buffet hangs on the wall, 17 inches above the floor, with a gridded wall unit above. Each door on the cabinet has a recessed metal washer as a door pull, but here's the fun part: You can insert a floral pick with a fresh flower into each washer, and the flat face of the cabinet becomes a sort of vase!

- I designed all of the lighting fixtures with Doug's piano-playing heritage in mind. In the dining room, the Garbo is a black fabric drum with three layers of beveled mirror "keys"—like piano keys! The light fixture over the piano is a campy version of a candelabra, with a white bird in a white cage. (There was already enough gold in the room, no need to gild the cage.)

RIGHT: This super-cool cabinet fits on the wall between the two windows and offers a ton of storage space for everything dining-related.

BELOW: In the dining room, which is actually much larger than the living room, upholstered chairs wear a large-scale damask in graphic black and white. The chandelier features a black fabric drum with beveled mirror rectangles that play on the theme of piano keys. A stylized chrome sconce mounted on each tall mirror simply plugs into a wall outlet, so no complicated wiring was needed. The mirrors double the light and add to the festive atmosphere.

FUN, FEMININE, AND FABULOUS

CHALLENGE

Nicola loves the beach cottage she calls home—except for the big room that is supposed to be her living and dining room. It's got great bones and loads of architectural character, with a dramatic coved ceiling, Mission-style paneling, and beautiful parquet floors. But all of the wood is stained dark brown, the windows are small and high, and there's only one small ceiling fixture to light the entire space. The room feels dark and masculine, more like a men's club than a place where a hip, fun, just-turned-40 woman would entertain her friends. And Nicola has lots of friends, so I have some work to do!

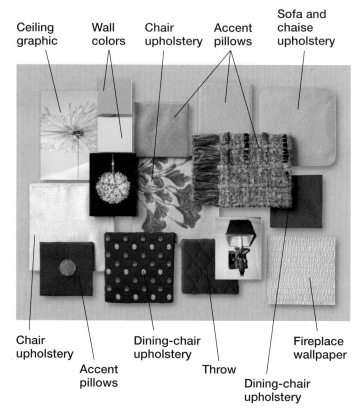

Ceiling graphic · Wall colors · Chair upholstery · Accent pillows · Sofa and chaise upholstery · Chair upholstery · Accent pillows · Dining-chair upholstery · Throw · Dining-chair upholstery · Fireplace wallpaper

BEFORE: With its dark paneling and parquet floors, this living and dining room felt like a depressing dungeon. It's the main floor of an otherwise bright and cheery duplex beach cottage that's been renovated from the top down—but the reno didn't reach this part of the house.

AFTER: I did the unthinkable—I painted the wood paneling—but what a difference it makes! Antique-white paint actually emphasizes the moldings and creates a light and airy background for a scheme of pink, white, and chocolate. It's feminine, flirty, and simply fantastic!

SOLUTION

- I know it's controversial to paint natural wood paneling, but Nicola wanted light and bright, and covering all of that dark wood with antique-white paint was the only way to get there.

- To give the living area a focal point, I built out a section of the wall and put in a new gas fireplace. It's a zero-clearance fireplace, a prefabricated unit that doesn't need a noncombustible surround, so I can turn the whole built-out section into a feature with wallpaper.

- Furniture divides the big space into two zones, one for the living area and the other for dining. A long sofa with a chaise component defines the living area, and a pair of English-inspired high-back chairs rounds out the seating group.

- Nicola loved her dining table, but the trestle base interfered with pulling chairs up to the ends. To seat more people, it needed some creative reworking: I removed the legs, base, and apron; added new corner supports; reattached the splayed legs; and added a new apron. Now the six new upholstered dining chairs can pull up comfortably all around.

- The room was sadly lacking in lighting, so I added recessed fixtures around the perimeter, a sparkly little crystal pendant in the living room, and a glamorous chrome chandelier to mark the dining area. Sconces that match the chandelier accent the end wall in the living room, tying the two spaces together.

RIGHT: Painting all the woodwork and the ceiling in antique white banished the dreary dungeon feeling and actually plays up the sculptural effect of the paneling. Building out a portion of the wall created a place to install a gas-insert fireplace and gives the living room a focal point. A fluffy shag rug anchors the seating group and puts toe-pleasing texture underfoot.

ABOVE: Nicola's beloved dining table underwent a little surgery to seat more people, and now six comfy barrel-back chairs can be drawn up for dinner parties. A contemporary chrome chandelier with chocolate fabric shades injects a little modern style to perk up the traditional architecture.

STYLE ELEMENTS

- Nicola loves pink and flowers, and I found the perfect upholstery fabric: a modern, graphic design with big agapanthus flowers on a light background. I used it to cover the two high-back chairs in the living area. A variety of accent fabrics in scrumptious textures and tones picks up on the pink and green in the floral.

- To add some personality in the dining area, I upholstered the barrel-back dining chairs in fun pink polka dots, with a solid brown silk on the fronts and seats. The brown relates to the parquet floor and helps ground all the light fabrics, so the look isn't too cutesy or girly.

- Opposite the new fireplace wall was the stairwell wall, which had no paneling. I painted it a fresh green to reflect one of the colors in the fabric (see pages 106 and 107). Then I upholstered the sofa and chaise in a glazed antique-white leather with a pearl finish to contrast very subtly with the wall.

- I covered the fireplace surround with a heavy wallpaper that has a crinkled-fabric quality. It adds a little shimmer and texture to the fireplace wall and sets off the floating hearth, which is made of reclaimed wood similar to Nicola's dining table. The hearth and stainless-steel fireplace surround both curve gently, picking up on the coved ceiling. The curved edges are even a little, dare I say, feminine?

- The ceiling is the fifth wall in any room, and it's a huge part of the character of this space. It needed something special, and I found just the thing: vinyl graphic transfers. An image of an agapanthus flower was enlarged onto the vinyl material and transferred to the ceiling with some firm rubbing. Scattered over the ceiling, the flowers look like hand-painted art and beautifully call attention to the coved surface.

RIGHT: The agapanthus fabric establishes the room's fresh palette and speaks to the natural setting outside. Sconces that match the dining area chandelier add intimate accent lighting at this end of the room.

ABOVE: The crystal pendant falls from the center of the ceiling art, a vinyl transfer image of an agapanthus flower inspired by the fabric and enlarged to the appropriate scale. I scattered more images randomly across the entire ceiling to call attention to this distinctive architectural feature.

RIGHT: The long sofa and chaise sit in front of the stairwell wall and the staircase leading to the basement. Bouclé, polka-dot, and solid pillows and a luscious quilted-velvet throw break up the expanse of solid color on the seating. The sparkly little pendant brings light down into the conversation grouping, and a funky pink-feather lamp is a fun and whimsical accent that also happens to be functional, giving Nicola a light to read by.

OPPOSITE: Access to the living area is through a glass-enclosed porch with a lovely view of the outdoors. Before, coming from the porch into the living-dining room had been like entering a cave. Now the light, bright, nature-inspired feeling of the porch continues indoors.

LEFT: Once Nicola's living room and dining room were transformed, the porch needed a little pick-me-up too! A comfy French-style armchair and a tripod table make this the perfect spot for morning coffee. Chocolate-brown woven-wood blinds provide privacy and light control when needed.

FAMILY CENTRAL

CHALLENGE

Mary's home is the headquarters for all of the family gatherings, so it's always packed with people. The problem is that the dining room can only seat six, and the living room is hard-pressed to accommodate even that many. Both rooms fall short in the storage department too. Mary likes the traditional style of her 1930s house, and she knows there's got to be a better way to deal with the space limitations than bringing in chairs from the bedrooms whenever people come over. Fortunately, I have some ideas that can help!

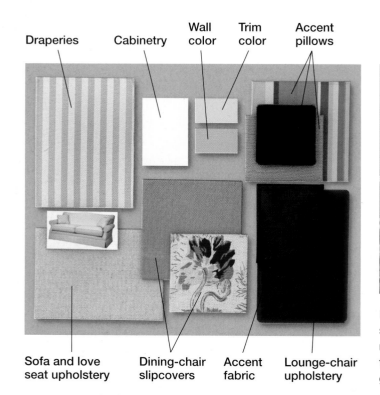

Draperies   Cabinetry   Wall color   Trim color   Accent pillows

Sofa and love seat upholstery   Dining-chair slipcovers   Accent fabric   Lounge-chair upholstery

BEFORE: Mary's dining room could barely handle her family of seven, but when they wanted to watch TV together in the living room, they had to crowd onto the sofa or spread out on the floor. And when the extended family descended for frequent gatherings, these two rooms weren't up to the task.

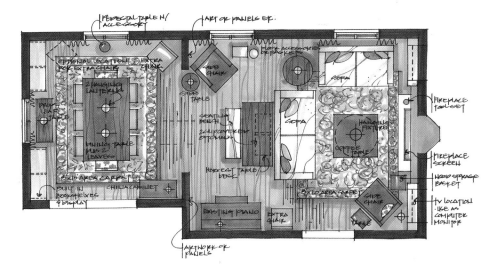

AFTER: New furniture, new color, and new fabrics create a family-friendly space for eating and relaxing. I kicked the style quotient up a notch to give Mary a dressier, more updated interpretation of traditional style, along with much better everyday function.

SOLUTION

- I started by ripping out the corner cabinets in the dining room and installing a wall of floor-to-ceiling cabinets. Four units are bolted to the wall for security and outfitted with glass shelves and mirrored backs. The mirrors create the illusion that the entire wall is windows.

- In the living room, the old 1930s built-in bookshelves were deep enough for books but couldn't handle the technology that comes with modern living. I pulled out the bookcases and replaced them with cabinetry that fills the old space and extends into the room to provide the depth needed for a new TV and media equipment.

- I reworked the fireplace to make it more of a feature in the new design scheme. A new, beefier mantel and surround give it much more prominence, and new drywall above provides a solid foundation for a big over-mantel mirror that expands the sense of space.

- There was no lighting to speak of in either room, and because the ceilings were plaster, I couldn't put in recessed lights. I managed to wrangle wiring for one new ceiling fixture in the living room, and that was no easy task! But I had to opt for wall sconces elsewhere. The solution actually worked to my advantage, because sconces not only minimize the damage to the plaster surfaces, but also provide intimate lighting and traditional style.

- To relieve crowding around the dining room table, I replaced Mary's small dining set with a new mahogany table on wheels. It comfortably seats six and can be extended with leaves. And when she really has a crowd, she can pull up a new drop-leaf table for a 16-foot-long dining area.

BELOW: The new table still seats 6, but it expands to 16 feet of dining area when the extensions are added and a drop-leaf table is pulled up to one end. Mirror backing on the new open cabinets creates the illusion of light coming in through a wall of windows.

ABOVE: A new mantel and surround, flanked by deeper bookcases, give the focal-point wall much more presence and make a strong statement of traditional style. Sconces beside the windows supply cozy overall lighting. A big mirror over the mantel doubles the impact of the sconces and the sparkly pendant fixture. Accent lights in the bookcases also help brighten the once-dark room.

STYLE ELEMENTS

- Updating the look of the living room started with new cabinetry. I used inexpensive paint-grade cabinetry and gave it the look of quality and traditional style with customized detailing: deep, classic-profile crown moldings; recessed-panel doors and sides; and a stepped return from the fireplace surround to the wall.

- Paint came to the rescue in both rooms, with a new bone color for the walls and vanilla for the trim, bookcases, and cabinets. To play up the bookcases in the living room, I painted the backs raspberry red—a pop of color that adds excitement to the space.

- New dining chairs (10 of them!) wear natural linen slipcovers for everyday use. Linen always has a wrinkly, lived-in look, which makes it perfect for an informal, traditional setting. I chose a vintage-inspired floral for the head chairs—it's forgiving and hides spills—and solid sage green for the remaining chairs. For more formal occasions, Mary can remove the slipcovers to reveal cream upholstery with nailhead trim.

- To add softness and depth to the walls, I framed each window with floor-to-ceiling draperies in a vanilla-and-taupe mini-stripe. Along with the bone-colored walls, the draperies form a neutral backdrop for the furniture at the center of each room. The stripe also grounds the floral and provides a sense of structure.

- The dining room chandelier is a classic traditional design, with electric candles, crystal bobeches, and wrought-iron arms. The sconces pick up on the black metal color and crystal detail, and the living room fixture plays off the same theme, with crystal beads and candle-flame bulbs in a curvy black metal cage. The living room pendant operates with a pull-cord, so it didn't have to be wired to a wall switch (whew!).

RIGHT: The piano needed to stay put in this corner, but I replaced the piano bench with a slipcovered chair that can double as a dining chair when there's a crowd for dinner.

BELOW: A solid bone-colored fabric on both major seating pieces relates them to the walls and keeps the room's overall feeling neutral and relaxed. Striped and solid pillows bring in accents of raspberry, chocolate, and sage, all drawn from the key floral fabric in the dining room.

FROM BLAND TO BEAUTIFUL

CHALLENGE

Pat admits that she's something of a design chicken—she's had the same beige-on-beige color scheme in her L-shaped living room and dining room for more than 20 years because it's safe. Now, however, she's going to be hosting her niece's wedding shower, and she wants to brighten things up a bit, maybe even shock her family and friends! I'm going to give her rooms a fresh new look, but I promise that it will also have the longevity she values.

BEFORE: After decades of living with this same brown wall-to-wall carpet, beige walls, and pink-and-green upholstery, Pat was ready for a change. The only thing she wanted to keep was the big teakwood wall unit, which had served her well for 30 years.

BEFORE: Pat's small, lackluster dining room was a dim passageway between the living room and the kitchen. Guests who sat at the ends bumped their knees on the table's deep apron, so the table wasn't as functional as it could be.

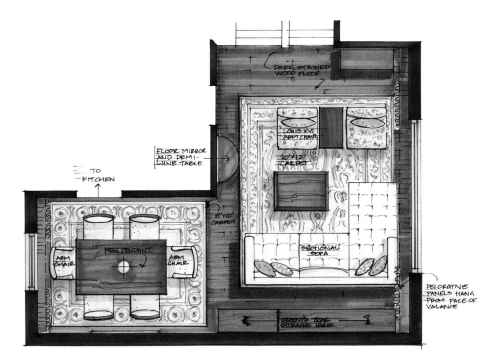

AFTER: Even the old teak bookshelves look revitalized now that the wall color, floors, and furnishings have been updated. The color scheme is still neutral but far from boring, with icy blue and teal accents that play up the warmth of the wood tones.

SOLUTION

- I started by pulling up that tired brown carpet to uncover the original hardwood floors. With a little refinishing and a rich walnut stain, they make a beautiful, medium-toned foundation for the new scheme.

- I wanted to ease Pat into color gently and give her a space she would be comfortable with, so I painted most of the walls a light, warm, buttery beige. It's still neutral, but it has a little more character than the old near-white walls. I gave two walls a special paint treatment to inject some unexpected elegance into both rooms.

- The teak unit fits on only one wall, so I worked around it and used it as the backdrop for an absolutely gorgeous chaise and sofa. This L-shaped piece provides lots of comfy seating and better fills the space. I also added a couple of armchairs to round out the seating in the living room.

ABOVE: The same draperies and sheers dress the small window in the dining room to unify the two spaces. New, more functional and comfortable furniture and more lighting bring the room up-to-date.

- Pat wanted to keep her old teak dining table, but the way it was constructed meant that whoever sat at the ends had to sit side-saddle. The new table allows chairs to be pulled all the way under the table—no more bruised knees! I also brought in a mix of upholstered and armless chairs, which can be moved into the living room when needed.

- The dining room window was fairly small, but in the living room the windows stretched almost all the way across one entire wall. To scale them down a bit, I hung a combination of sheers and draperies and mounted the draperies on the valance instead of behind it. It's a good way to soften this hard feature, which is so common in houses of this vintage.

- Neither room had much in the way of lighting, so I went for a new record, installing twelve pot lights—eight in the living room and four in the dining room! It seems like a lot, but the adjustable fixtures let me spotlight several features and really play up the draperies and the teak wall unit.

- In the dining room, I replaced the single ceiling fixture with a long, four-light chandelier. Installed about 30 inches above the table (60 inches above the floor), it sheds light evenly over the entire table but isn't in the way when you stand up.

BELOW: A beautiful new chaise and sectional sofa now anchor the living room, with Pat's beloved teak bookcases as a backdrop. Restyling the arrangement of objects in and on the teak wall unit turned it into a showcase for Pat's books and collections—and gave me another opportunity to introduce small doses of color into the room. The absolutely fabulous draperies make the biggest color statement, which I repeated in the pillows and rug for emphasis.

STYLE ELEMENTS

- The inspiration for the entire color scheme came from one of my favorite sweaters—I loved the way the fake fur trim blended undertones of creamy beige with gray-blue and icy blue, so I used those tones for the wall colors, draperies, and accents. It just goes to show, you never know where inspiration will come from!

- To pick up on the wall color, I covered the windows with an incredible champagne-colored crinkled silk sheer. Then I framed the sheers with draperies made from the most amazing iridescent blue silk. It's pre-sewn to look button-tufted and adds a real sense of luxury to the rooms.

- The drapery fabric inspired an equally gorgeous iridescent paint treatment on two accent walls. Venetian plaster is a tricky and time-consuming process that involves priming and base-coating the walls with two coats of paint. That leaves a toothy, somewhat rough surface for the smooth plaster coat. Finally, a top coat of gel medium mixed with metallic paint is troweled on to give a glowing iridescent effect that matches the silk draperies.

- The whole look I was after in Pat's living room was casual, soft, and elegant, so I chose a sectional and chaise that combine contemporary, clean, straight lines with traditional tufting on the seat cushions. Two antique Louis XVI chairs bring in the timeless elegance that Pat likes. For the dining room furniture, I selected chairs and a table with the same long, tapered, sleek legs, but the woods are different, so the furniture doesn't look too matched.

ABOVE: To add real drama to Pat's new rooms, I finished the entry wall in a super-elegant Venetian plaster paint treatment that exactly matches the color of the draperies. The treatment continues around the corner into the dining area. A tall mirror brings more light into the space. The demilune accent table picks up on the dark mahogany stain of the coffee table and the dining room table; these touches of dark wood really anchor the light color scheme and play up the beauty of that blue wall finish.

- Area carpets bring in lots of soft, subdued color in both rooms and anchor the two areas. In the dining room, a medallion carpet lends itself to having furniture centered on it. In the living room, the allover pattern means you're not committed to just one furniture arrangement.

- Pat had a group of watercolors that I reframed as a series to give them more dramatic impact. A new beige mat with a blue liner pulls out the color in the paintings and picks up on the room's new color scheme.

OPPOSITE: A pair of antique French armchairs balances the sofa and chaise at the entry to the room. I hung the shimmery button-tufted silk drapery panels on a rod mounted on the fixed valance to soften that architectural element. A recessed light in the ceiling is positioned to wash light down on the draperies, highlighting the texture and iridescent color.

URBAN COUNTRY OASIS

CHALLENGE

The best thing about Lana and Steven's living-dining room combo is the view—a spectacular panorama overlooking a wooded ravine. Unfortunately, that view is framed by ugly pink draperies unflatteringly highlighted by fluorescent lights. Too-short dining room curtains, stained and dirty wall-to-wall carpeting, and a hideous sofa are other "perks" that came with the house when they bought it. Lana and Steven are in the process of renovating the entire 1950s ranch house, but they are pressed for time to get this big dual-purpose room in shape for Lana's upcoming 40th-birthday celebration. They've asked me to help them transform it into the ultimate entertaining space.

Mantel and cabinetry   Club-chair upholstery   Dining chair seat upholstery   Draperies   Sheers

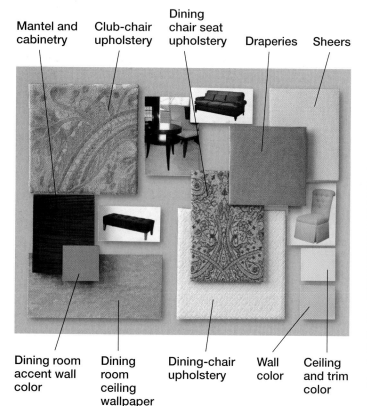

Dining room accent wall color   Dining room ceiling wallpaper   Dining-chair upholstery   Wall color   Ceiling and trim color

BEFORE: With a mishmash of nice and take-me-to-the-dumpster furnishings and a jumble of patterns and colors, Lana and Steven's living-dining room lacked style and comfort. The beautiful view was its main redeeming virtue, and they liked the huge granite fireplace too.

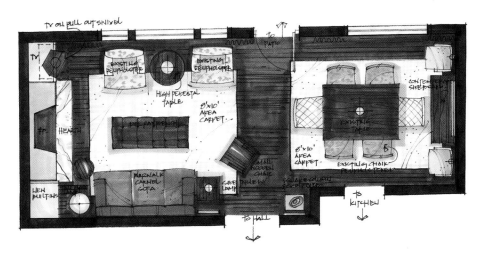

AFTER: A new, earthy taupe color scheme inspired by the fireplace unifies the entire space with rich, subtle sophistication. I reworked some of Lana and Steven's furniture to better suit the new space and replaced the dowdy old draperies with luxurious new panels and sheers—a treatment worthy of the view outside!

SOLUTION

- Ripping up the wall-to-wall carpeting revealed a goldmine: the original gorgeous oak floors. Refinished to their former glory, the floors laid the groundwork for the nature-inspired oasis I had in mind.

- The fireplace was a dominant feature in the room, and Lana and Steven liked it—but they wished it had a mantel for hanging Christmas stockings. I added a floating mantel shelf to take care of the stockings and installed cabinetry on either side of the fireplace to provide much-needed storage. The 48-inch-tall solid oak cabinets keep baby David's toys out of sight on one side and keep the TV and media equipment handy but hidden on the other.

- To bring out the color of the stone (and make it easier to clean off soot), I applied a sealer and color enhancer to the fireplace.

- The room had no lighting except for fluorescent strips in the valance. I eliminated the fluorescents and installed recessed lighting throughout the space, as well as sconces and a chandelier in the dining room.

- Installing the chandelier created a teeny bit of a problem. A junction box needed to be moved so the chandelier could be centered over the dining table, and that left a hole in the old stucco ceiling. I'll do just about anything to avoid having to redo a stucco ceiling, and I came up with a pretty fabulous solution here: a 7 x 9-foot canopy that creates the effect of a dropped ceiling over the dining table. Built out of plywood and covered with wallpaper, it definitely says "city sophistication."

ABOVE: A comfy chenille sofa suits the scale of the room and is both kid- and adult-friendly. The leather ottoman does triple duty as a coffee table, a place to prop tired feet, and extra seating for Lana's birthday crowd.

- Lana and Steven's two club chairs were in good condition and in scale with the space, so I simply reupholstered them. But the old sofa went to sofa heaven, and I brought in a new, more contemporary one better suited to the room.

- In the dining area, I kept Lana and Steven's lovely Queen Anne dining table and side chairs, but I replaced the head chairs with dressy upholstered ones. And to break up the formality and too-matched look of a suite, I exchanged the Queen Anne china cabinet for a contemporary one in a similar dark-wood tone.

ABOVE: New cabinetry makes the fireplace wall even more of a feature and adds function too, with storage for the TV on one side and toys on the other. Sealer applied to the granite intensifies the stone's natural colors, which inspired the entire color scheme.

STYLE ELEMENTS

- The colors in the granite fireplace gave me the perfect jumping-off point for fabric and wall colors. A pinky taupe for the walls, mocha for an accent wall, and cream for the ceilings and trim make up a soft, understated palette that lets the view be the design story.

- To appropriately frame that view, I chose a beautiful, shimmery wool-silk blend for the drapery panels in both the living room and the dining room. Sheers with a pinky tinge and a subtle linen texture control the light and can be pulled back to reveal the splendid scenery.

- I reupholstered the two old club chairs in a classic champagne-colored damask with a pinky undertone. The damask speaks to the traditional side of things, while a new sofa in chenille brings in a more casual, contemporary look. A tufted-leather coffee table/ottoman bridges the two styles.

- In the dining room, the dropped canopy gives the room a sophisticated urban edge thanks to the incredible handmade metallic wallpaper I used to cover it. Because the plywood base was rough, it had to be covered with liner paper first to hide imperfections (but not the hole for the wiring!). After the canopy was raised and secured to the ceiling, the handmade wallpaper was applied in squares, and the sides were trimmed with crown molding.

- Along with the weathered-metal look of the wallpaper, Lucite-and-mirror sconces and a coordinating chandelier inject the contemporary accents needed to balance the traditional furnishings in the dining room.

ABOVE: I moved the armchairs of the dining set to the back wall, just in case Lana and Steven need extra seating at the table or in the living room. A simple sideboard replaced the old china cabinet for a cleaner, more modern look. A big mirror propped on the table reflects the ceiling canopy and chandelier, and I layered a painting over it for extra interest.

OPPOSITE: Lana and Steven were so pleased with the renovation of their kitchen that they opened up the wall to the dining room so the spaces could flow better. To play up the weathered-metal look of the wallpaper on the ceiling canopy, I accented the meeting points with metal screw covers. An allover patterned area rug anchors the dining area—note that it's big enough for all of the seating to fit on it even when the chairs are pulled out.

MODERN VISION

CHALLENGE

Andrew's career has kept him moving from city to city, but now he's ready to put down roots. He has bought his dream home, a 1950s split-level on a golf course, and has begun making plans for renovating it. First room on the list: the big, incredibly pink living room, which just happens to have the best view of the outdoors! Andrew loves golf, and he also loves design. He'd like this room and the tiny adjoining dining room to be a spectacular, masculine, ultra-hip space for entertaining. Access to the outdoors and the golf course would be a major plus.

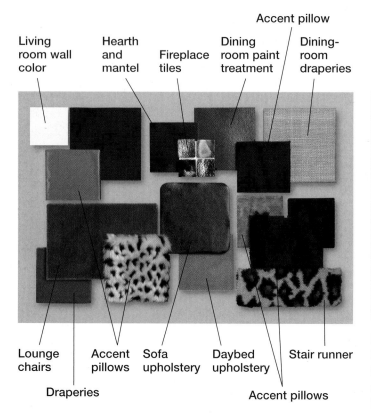

Living room wall color · Hearth and mantel · Fireplace tiles · Dining room paint treatment · Accent pillow · Dining-room draperies

Lounge chairs · Draperies · Accent pillows · Sofa upholstery · Daybed upholstery · Accent pillows · Stair runner

BEFORE: Bubblegum-pink walls and a young, hip, golf-loving bachelor simply do not mix. The puny fireplace with its traditional-style surround didn't make much of an impression either. The best thing about the room was the view overlooking the 16th hole of the golf course!

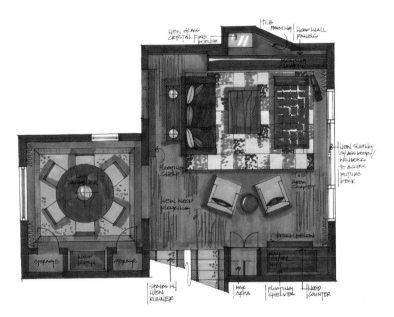

AFTER: Modern, masculine, and super-cool, the living room now functions as a show-stopping place to entertain old friends and new colleagues. New sliding glass doors not only open up the view but also will connect to a future deck.

ABOVE: Removing the old fireplace wall back to the exterior brick enabled me to create a trough between the ceiling and the new fireplace. That's where I installed spotlights to wash dramatic light down the new surfaces of horizontal wood planking and textured medium-density fiberboard (MDF).

SOLUTION

- The house had great bones and lots of space, but this room and the dining room needed to be totally reinvented to make them work for Andrew. He wanted the fireplace to be a dramatic focal point, so I teed off by ripping out the fireplace wall all the way back to the brick exterior. I designed a stunning new raised fireplace that stretches about 10 feet along the wall but still makes use of the existing chimney.

- Next, I cut a 12-foot opening in the window wall and replaced the windows with patio doors to the future deck. By next spring, Andrew will be able to get to the outdoors and the golf course from this room.

- On the wall opposite the fireplace, I installed a tall storage cabinet, long shelves, and a counter that can double as a home office and a buffet for parties. The cabinet incorporates storage for refreshments as well as office supplies. Mirror backing behind the open shelves reflects light and outdoor views and adds to the illusion of space.

- To bring the lighting in these rooms up to par, I designed a combination of practical and special-effects lighting. A chandelier in the dining room and recessed ceiling fixtures in the living room take care of the practical part. For the special effects, a compact pendant hovers over the coffee table, and spotlights installed in a trough in front of the fireplace wall rake light down the new textured surfaces.

- Andrew wanted to pipe music from elsewhere in the house down to these rooms, so I found the coolest-ever concealed speakers. You set them between the wall studs and plaster over them, so they're completely out of sight. A control panel in the wall brings in the music. Amazing!

- In the tiny dining room, I refinished the floors to more closely match the dark stain of the existing living room floors. A new paint treatment and a mirrored ceiling turn this space into a phenomenal showpiece of a room, a cozy and elegant place for dinner and conversation.

RIGHT: On the back wall, a tall storage cabinet accommodates both office supplies and refreshments. Long floating shelves provide display space, with a counter for doing paperwork below. An entire mirrored wall behind the shelves doubles light and views. New sliding doors lead to a future deck.

STYLE ELEMENTS

- The pink paint rapidly disappeared under a fresh coat of crisp white in the living room. In the dining room, I covered the old pink and gray walls with a stunning metallic bronze strié finish. It's a multi-step process that starts with a brown base coat, followed by a coat of gold metallic paint and then a deep brown glaze that's rolled on over the wall. Dragging a wallpaper brush through the wet glaze gives the strié finish.

- The key to the look Andrew wanted in the living room was to combine clean, contemporary, pared-down design elements with natural ones such as rich, dark-wood surfaces and polished stone in a linear, controlled, refined way. That's exactly what I did with the fireplace. Dark-stained wide wood planks applied horizontally to the new drywall stretch across about three-quarters of the wall, creating a dramatic, asymmetrical focal point.

- The firebox for the new gas fireplace is clad with iridescent glass tiles that continue beyond the fire area to the exterior wall. Black composite granite frames the firebox and is cantilevered to create the extended hearth and mantel. Instead of the usual ceramic logs, I opted for special cut-glass pieces for the fuel for a unique, ultra-modern look.

- On the remaining wall beside the fireplace, I installed MDF and applied a textured treatment that contrasts with the smooth wood and shows off a grouping of African masks.

- To soften the stark, contemporary lines, I brought in loads of yummy fabrics—velvets, fun faux leopard fur, and antique chenille for accents; rich leather for seating; and the most incredible metallic silver fabric for the draperies—truly, it's like liquid pewter, just scrumptious, and it frames the sliding doors without covering the view. For a high-style covering on the stairs, I laid down a hardwearing leopard-print runner that makes a great introduction to this über-cool space.

- Andrew needed all-new furniture, since the pieces he had in the room were castoffs he'd found in the garage! A sleek black leather sofa and modern lounge chairs establish the hip, modern look. On the third "wall" of the conversation area I positioned an orange leather daybed—it provides lots of room for seating without blocking the view to the outdoors. In the dining room, a round table is ideal for such a small space because you can squeeze more people around it.

RIGHT: Exquisite liquid-pewter metallic draperies frame the new sliding-glass doors without blocking the view. The molded-glass coffee table provides loads of function but doesn't take up any visual space. An array of touchable textures keeps the sleek, modern furniture from feeling hard and cold.

BELOW: The pass-through to the kitchen was already in place, so I emphasized the asymmetrical composition of the wall with a long dark-wood shelf that serves as display and buffet space. Recessed fixtures in the ceiling provide overall lighting, and spotlights in the trough above the fireplace play up the art and textures on this focal-point wall.

RIGHT: What looks like a paneled wall in the dining room proves to be the door to a handy storage cupboard.

OPPOSITE: A mirrored ceiling makes this little dining room feel two stories high. The dark paint treatment, a metallic bronze strié, gives the room an incredibly rich, masculine feel, like an exclusive men's club. The leopard-print rug speaks to the runner on the stairs nearby, and the mirrored buffet, set into an existing niche, enlarges the apparent space with more reflections.

WORLD-CLASS VIEW

CHALLENGE

Globe-trotting travelers Carol and Helmet have finally found their dream home: a gorgeous two-story penthouse with soaring ceilings, big open-concept spaces, and spectacular light and views. Although they're thrilled to have a place that's nearly twice the size of their old home, they've discovered that their old furniture doesn't work very well in the new great room—it's too small in proportion to the scale of the space. They'd like this room to reflect their travels and experiences and to be as wonderful inside as their view of the world outside.

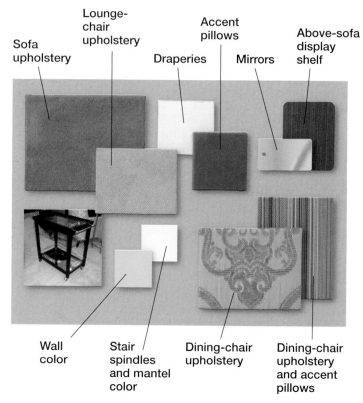

Sofa upholstery
Lounge-chair upholstery
Draperies
Accent pillows
Mirrors
Above-sofa display shelf
Wall color
Stair spindles and mantel color
Dining-chair upholstery
Dining-chair upholstery and accent pillows

BEFORE: Carol and Helmet's penthouse suite boasted beautiful floors, newly painted walls, and fantastic light and views, but the space was so big that their old furniture looked lost.

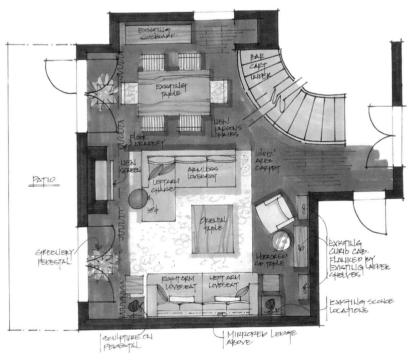

AFTER: Large-scale furniture and art tame the super-sized space and make it feel welcoming and comfortable. I painted the oak spindles on the staircase to match the trim for a fresher, more contemporary look.

SOLUTION

- I didn't need to paint the walls because Carol and Helmet had just had it done, and they loved the soft, buttery color. The oak staircase, however, felt dark and heavy, so I painted the colonial-style spindles white to match the trim. I also painted the over-mantel white to give the small fireplace more visual weight.

- The high arched windows are a blessing and a curse—they let in wonderful light, but all that sun also means a lot of heat, and it fades the furniture. To give Carol and Helmet some control over the sunlight streaming in, I installed vertical blinds that operate by remote control. You can even tilt the shades according to the angle of the sun.

- To unify the arched windows with the French doors and windows below, I hung four dummy panels of sheers that fall 20 feet to the floor. Talk about drama! The panels are tied to medallions installed in the ceiling in line with the ledge so they fall in one long, uninterrupted column.

- Big spaces need big furniture. I replaced the couple's leather sofa with two love seats put together (one with a right arm, one with a left arm) to give them 9 feet of seating against the wall. Balancing this major piece are a chaise and an armless loveseat with a hefty Chinese-style coffee table in the center. A giant new rug pulls the living room seating together.

- To add lots of interest and sparkle to one of the soaring walls, I designed three frameless mirrors, 200 pounds each, to hang in a column and capture the views. Hoisting these puppies into place was a major feat of engineering, calling for 16 feet of scaffolding, 100 feet of rope, and a bunch of big, strong, burly men! Each mirror hangs on a French cleat, so it's not going anywhere.

RIGHT: To break up one huge wall and give it some visual interest, I designed three massive, frameless mirrors to hang on cleats. Reflecting light and views, they bring in sparkle and shine and create the illusion of still more windows on the world. A shelf under the bottom mirror provides room for display.

BELOW: Contemporary upholstered seating suited to the scale of the space defines the new living area. Simple sheers hanging from the 20-foot-high ceiling help soften the architecture and bring lots of drama to the room.

STYLE ELEMENTS

- It's always a challenge to transition old furniture into a new space, especially if the new space is a different style. Carol and Helmet really wanted to keep their antique dining room set, but all that dark-stained wood seemed very heavy in the light, bright space. Replacing the chairs with contemporary upholstered ones created a more eclectic look and brought color and pattern into the dining area.

- The dining chair fabrics combine a creamy, buttery background that speaks to the wall color with camel and sage accents that I carried over to the living room in pillows. For the new upholstery and rug in the living area, I chose a soft, earthy palette that harmonizes with the walls.

- The old fixture in the dining room was all wrong for the space—it directed light upward, which just accentuated the height of the ceiling, and the dark wrought iron was much too traditional and visually heavy. I replaced it with a contemporary one designed exactly for rooms like this, where traditional and contemporary styles play off each other. The crystal and polished chrome are contemporary materials and the nine-arm form is traditional, so the piece bridges the style gap and makes the antique table look even better. A companion fixture hangs in the stairwell.

- The deep ledge dividing the upper and lower windows is the perfect place to showcase the couple's large-scale art and artifacts. I also filled the walls with some of their travel photos, matted in extra-wide white mats and framed in black to make them stand out as art pieces.

ABOVE: Extra-wide white mats and black frames showcase Carol and Helmet's travel photos above the sideboard. Polished chrome accent lamps play off the dark finish of the antique sideboard and bring more sparkle to this corner of the room.

OPPOSITE: An entire matched suite of furniture can look stagnant, so I like to break things up by mixing a traditional table with upholstered chairs. The sparkle of a contemporary chrome and crystal chandelier balances the visual weight of the dark-toned furniture, and the chocolate-hued fabric shades speak back to the wood of the table and tie the two together.

STRIKING A BALANCE

CHALLENGE

Philippe's 100-year-old house had been divided into three apartments, one of which he lived in while he rented the other two. Now that he and Sara are married, they're turning his triplex into their one-plex—which can be complex! They have gutted the entire building and are gradually putting it back together to make a single-family home where they can look forward to hearing the pitter-patter of tiny feet (and I'm not talking about dogs!). They have completed a few rooms but could really use some help finishing off the main living space on the first floor.

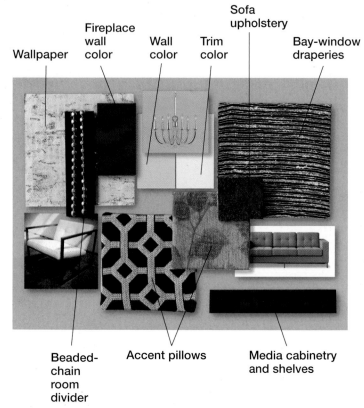

Wallpaper

Fireplace wall color

Wall color

Trim color

Sofa upholstery

Bay-window draperies

Beaded-chain room divider

Accent pillows

Media cabinetry and shelves

BEFORE: Philippe and Sara took the entire first floor back to the studs and had finished the kitchen at the back of the house when they called on me for help. The room that was to be their living and dining space was an empty shell in need of everything.

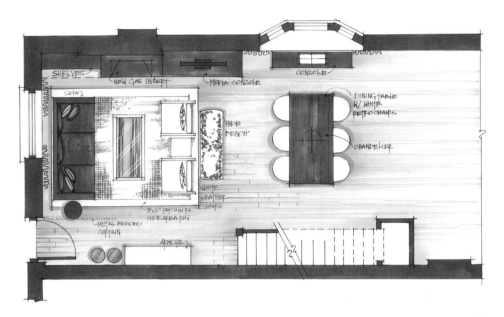

AFTER: Long ropes of ball chain create a privacy screen for the living area to separate it from the entry. To please Sara's modern tastes as well as Philippe's desire to reference the house's age, I balanced the sleek-and-chic, mostly modern makeover with rustic touches, including wallpaper that looks like birch bark and a natural-wood coffee table. A color scheme of charcoal, white, and amber and an array of contrasting textures create a rich, sophisticated room.

BELOW: Low, modern seating lets the eye flow without interruption all the way back to the kitchen, which helps the narrow room feel more expansive. The exposed-brick wall provided the cue for light maple flooring. A modern, "pixilated" area rug pulls all of the room's colors together.

SOLUTION

- Philippe and Sara's house is a long, narrow building with an exposed-brick wall on one side and a bay window that is literally within arm's reach of the neighbor's house on the other. The exposed brick gives the space that great vintage vibe that Philippe loves, so I used it as my jumping-off point for the room's design.

- I had the surface of the brick ground down to give it a nice, smooth finish and sealed it to get rid of dust.

- The front door brings you right into the living area, so I created a privacy panel at the entry with a ceiling-mounted track of silver ball chains that fall straight to the floor. It's a great solution for a small space because it defines boundaries without blocking sight lines through the room.

- On the outside wall, I boxed in the ductwork and built out a portion of the wall for a new gas fireplace. The fireplace insert is raised off the floor, which has two benefits: one, it's easier to see from anywhere in the room, and two, it's safer when there could be babies exploring this space.

- On each side of the fireplace, new cabinetry and floating shelves provide storage for media, a spot for the TV, and room for display. (One pair of shelves lines up nicely with the top of the fireplace, creating visual continuity.) To give the shelves a floating effect, a skeleton framework of 1 x 1-inch wood strips is bolted to the wall first, and the shelf, built like a hollow shell, slips snugly over it.

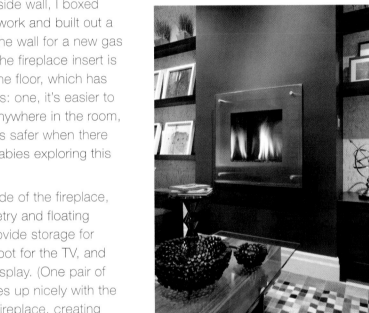

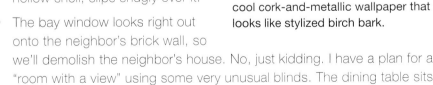

ABOVE: A sleek, contemporary fireplace anchors the living area, flanked by floating shelves and media cabinetry in an espresso stain. For the balancing rustic touch, I covered the walls with a cool cork-and-metallic wallpaper that looks like stylized birch bark.

- The bay window looks right out onto the neighbor's brick wall, so we'll demolish the neighbor's house. No, just kidding. I have a plan for a "room with a view" using some very unusual blinds. The dining table sits in front of that window, with a chandelier above.

- Since I was starting from scratch, I could install lots of recessed fixtures in the ceiling to provide all the ambient light the room needs.

STYLE ELEMENTS

- To pick up the yellow tones of the exposed brick wall, I laid down prefinished maple flooring that flows perfectly into the kitchen cabinet color they've already installed.

- As the focal point of the living area, the fireplace is very modern, with a wide, stainless-steel front and polished pebbles instead of logs in the firebox.

- With such a modern fireplace, I wanted the wall beside it to be more rustic. I found the perfect wallpaper: white-painted cork backed with foil—it looks like birch bark! The natural lines and cracks disguise the fact that the cork is in squares, so the effect on the wall is completely seamless. It's natural and rustic-looking, yet a little bit modern with that metallic backing.

- For seating, I went with modern pieces that will please Sara and provide lots of comfort in a small space. A boxy three-seater sofa has the long, low profile and stainless-steel legs of a modern piece, combined with tufting for a nod to tradition. It's upholstered in a felt-like charcoal fabric that's soft, fuzzy, and family-friendly.

- Two low, modern chairs with sleek stainless-steel frames keep the sofa company. In an open-concept space like this, I wanted something low to let the eye flow through the room. A big ottoman covered in cowhide and a coffee table made from a thick slab of wood add natural texture to balance the stainless steel.

- In the bay window, I installed a shade printed with a modern graphic pattern that gives this area visual interest and hides the neighbor's wall. I flanked the windows with the yummiest fabric, a textured stripe on a charcoal background. It looks very organic, almost like a strié. The fabric has a beautiful hand, but it's a little sheer, so I lined it with black dim-out fabric to give it a more opaque quality.

- The dining area captures what the design is all about: mixing Philippe's and Sara's styles. Dining room chairs inspired by mid-century modern designs surround a rustic barn-board table. Above it, I hung a chandelier that combines modern materials with cleaned-up traditional lines, and the whole area is grounded by the graphic window blinds.

RIGHT: The space-expanding lattice design on the window shades covers up an unfortunate view of a brick wall. Luscious draperies frame the window and soften the architecture.

OPPOSITE: A salvaged barn-board table paired with pedestal chairs inspired by Eero Saarinen's iconic 1950s Tulip chairs summarizes the whole concept of this space—a marriage of modern and rustic styles. The chrome chandelier is a contemporary take on traditional style, combining modern materials with a classic shape. Note the beaded chains draping the arms—they stand in for what would be crystal on an antique fixture and pick up on the privacy screen at the entry.

GLOBAL INSPIRATION

CHALLENGE

Jyoti is an airline pilot who loves her high-pressure job but also looks forward to coming home to decompress and entertain friends. Unfortunately, the living and dining rooms of her 100-year-old house don't lend themselves to relaxing or hosting a crowd. They are dark, dated, and claustrophobic, and the living room is dominated by an ugly brick fireplace that doesn't even work. Jyoti longs for a space that is light and bright, with more room for welcoming her friends. So I climbed into the pilot's seat to take these rooms to new heights of elegance!

Draperies

Wall color

Accent wall color

Accent pillows

Sofa and love-seat upholstery

Bench upholstery

BEFORE: A bulky brick fireplace that didn't work loomed large in the small living room, and the wall dividing the hall from the dining room made that space feel dark and cramped. Jyoti didn't care for the old-fashioned stained-glass windows and golden-oak floors and woodwork either.

AFTER: Now the living room and dining room are a warm and welcoming landing pad for this busy airline pilot. I completely reworked the fireplace wall to make it more functional with built-in storage and seating. The new gas-insert fireplace takes up much less space than the old non-functioning brick construction.

SOLUTION

- To open up the space and eliminate the dark, cramped feeling, I started by knocking down the knee wall at the entry and tearing out the long wall that divided the hall from the dining room. A short section of load-bearing wall needed to stay in place for structural reasons, and it helps mark the division between the two rooms.

- The biggest transformation came from tearing out the old fireplace and covering the two small, decorative windows above it. I completely reconfigured that entire wall by building in two floor-to-ceiling, 18-inch-deep cabinetry units with a built-in banquette between them. Deep drawers in the base of the banquette provide storage.

- On the wall above the banquette, I installed a super-cool flat-panel TV that looks like a framed mirror when the TV is turned off.

- In the cabinet unit closest to the dining room, I put in a shallow gas-insert fireplace, installing it at eye level so it can be enjoyed from both rooms. The other cabinet offers display space above and storage for media equipment below.

- To make the living room more comfortable for a crowd, I brought in an 84-inch-long three-seater sofa that sits right in front of the window. A miniature version, a 58-inch-long love seat, faces it. Because the doors in Jyoti's old house are narrow, I had the sofas constructed in three pieces so they'd fit through the entrance. Then I just had to reattach the arm sections to the body and plump the seat and back cushions into place.

- In the dining room, I replaced Jyoti's small dining set with a big double-pedestal table that can expand to seat as many as 12. The pedestal style is perfect for maximizing the number of people you can gather around the table because no one has to straddle a table leg.

- Knocking down a few walls helped open up the space, but lighting is really the key to the light, bright feeling Jyoti wanted. Recessed fixtures in the ceiling wash light down the walls and provide overall illumination. A crystal chandelier and sconces sparkle in the dining room, and in the entry, little beaded orbs flanking a console and mirror instantly say, "Welcome home."

LEFT: A big new table comfortably seats 6 and can expand to handle 12 guests, so Jyoti can entertain her many friends in style. A traditional crystal chandelier and sconces create a special-occasion feeling with lots of sparkle and shine.

ABOVE: In place of the bulky old fireplace, an upholstered banquette anchors the U-shaped seating group. I unified the new wall of storage with simple crown molding and a coat of crisp white paint for a clean, contemporary feeling, but instead of white or glass shelves, I used wood stained to match the floors. The natural tone complements the eclectic handcrafts that Jyoti collects. A drum-shaped wooden stool that mimics a Chinese garden stool serves as a side table but can double as seating when there's a crowd.

ABOVE: Replacing the long wall that enclosed the dining room with a narrower load-bearing section gives the room a lot more breathing space—and more room for a proper table and comfy chairs for entertaining. The soft vanilla wall color plays up the statement-making draperies and contrasts subtly with the crisp white baseboards and ceiling detail. Dark-stained hardwood floors anchor this lighter, brighter look and give it a contemporary edge.

STYLE ELEMENTS

- To reflect Jyoti's life as a high-flying world traveler, I chose a punchy red-and-cream ikat fabric as my starting point. This global pattern, found from Indonesia to South America, is a character builder in these rooms and provides the key to the color scheme. I pulled out the soft vanilla in the fabric for the wall color in the dining room and living room and used the bold red to bring some drama to the stair wall. Crisp white unifies the new cabinetry and seating niche in the living room and highlights the deep baseboards and dining room ceiling detail.

- With all of the walls and ceilings now light and bright, I anchored the whole area with a darker floor, an exotic African hardwood that is traditionally used in boat building. Its tighter grain looks more contemporary than the old golden-oak floors, and it promises Jyoti a creak-free, splinter-free surface underfoot.

- I framed the windows in each room with generous, 90-inch-long panels of the ikat. To complement the statement fabric, I chose a super-durable contemporary stripe for the banquette that pulls in the red and cream as well as the brown of the floor. A beautiful bark brown microfiber covers the sofa and love seat and picks up on the floor color as well.

- Accent pillows in a selection of primitive stripes, geometrics, and even a Persian design bring in global flavor and speak back to the ikat. For a personalized custom touch, I had a Persian motif scanned into a computer and then machine-stitched in brown and white on a red fabric for a pair of accent pillows.

- For light control and privacy, I hung simple white cellular shades in the windows.

RIGHT: With clean-lined, contemporary furniture as the bones of the room, accent pieces like this Chinese-style table bring in an eclectic, global character that speaks to Jyoti's wide-ranging experiences as a pilot. The table's slim proportions are perfect for a small space, and it's just the right height to serve as a sofa table behind the love seat.

RENOVATION TO THE RESCUE

CHALLENGE

Carl and Tony are the life of the neighborhood, hosting everything from street parties to summer barbecues and road-hockey games. When word got out that the pair was thinking of moving to a bigger house, the neighbors rose up in protest and begged them to stay—they even commissioned a beautiful leaded-glass window signed by everyone on the street. How could Carl and Tony say no? But remodeling their dark, dated, and too-small main floor is a bigger job than they can handle—and that's where I come in. I'm going to create a brighter, bigger, airier space that's more conducive to entertaining their favorite people: the friends on their street.

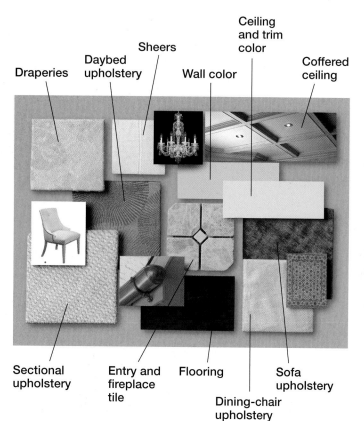

Draperies

Daybed upholstery

Sheers

Wall color

Ceiling and trim color

Coffered ceiling

Sectional upholstery

Entry and fireplace tile

Flooring

Dining-chair upholstery

Sofa upholstery

BEFORE: Carl and Tony's semi-detached Craftsman bungalow had lots of character, but the chopped-up spaces, angled ceilings, and small windows made it feel cramped and dark. The brick fireplace was an eyesore that they never used.

AFTER: Tearing out all the walls and reconfiguring the ceilings created a big, airy, open space that's bright and welcoming. Traditional trim work and details honor the age of the house, but the new color scheme gives the room a fresh, modern feeling. A new gas fireplace that turns on with the flick of a wall switch anchors the living area.

SOLUTION

- I had two priorities: Add more usable space and bring in more light. That meant lots of demolition: taking out walls to create one large, open-concept space; tearing out the angled ceilings; and enclosing the old porch. Five new Craftsman-style windows on the front and side of the enclosed porch flood the new space with light. At the entry, I installed the beautiful leaded-glass window that the neighbors had commissioned— it's the perfect spot to honor the close friendships that persuaded Carl and Tony to stay put!

- Pulling down the solid wall that had enclosed the staircase and replacing it with wrought-iron railings also added to the more open feeling of the space.

- The old fireplace was ugly and seldom used, so I tore it out and built out the wall to accommodate a new gas-insert fireplace with cabinetry on either side.

- Carl and Tony enjoyed watching TV in their old living room, but they didn't want the television to dominate the new space. So I installed a new flat-panel TV above the fireplace and hid all the wiring and hardware in the adjacent media cabinet. Then I used my favorite solution for working a TV into a very traditional space: I paired it with a framed piece of art that glides up out of the way with a remote control.

- One thing the old dining room lacked was adequate storage for all of Carl and Tony's crystal and china. I designed a new hutch with a quartz top for food service and plenty of cabinets and drawers for storage and display.

- In the large new living room, I divided the space into two conversation groups bridged by a luxurious daybed. It's a perfect place for one person to stretch out and watch TV or for a bunch of friends to gather for conversation and cocktails.

LEFT: On the back wall of the new space, a beautiful built-in hutch with deep, traditional crown moldings shows off Carl and Tony's crystal and china. I backed the glass shelves with mirrors to capture and reflect more light back into the room, and when you're standing in the living area, the mirrors create the illusion of additional windows along the back wall.

ABOVE: Taking out the stairway wall enhanced the sense of spaciousness, and a new wrought-iron railing respects the historical character of the house while introducing a lighter look. A big armoire serves as a coat closet and balances the fireplace.

ABOVE: Marble tile frames the new gas fireplace on all four sides for a cleaner look. To work a TV into the room in an unobtrusive way, I installed it behind a framed painting over the mantel. The painting disappears at the touch of a button to reveal the television. I kept the old stained-glass windows but integrated them better into the whole elevation with handsome, richly detailed cabinetry.

STYLE ELEMENTS

- To give the new space architectural character in keeping with the old house, I put in coffered ceilings, traditional crown molding, and tons of beautiful traditional detailing on all of the new built-in cabinets, mantel, and fireplace surround.

- A new floor of wide-plank, prefinished walnut has a hand-chiseled finish that gives it an aged, been-here-forever quality that anchors the elegant new look.

- For the entry vestibule, I laid down a durable, waterproof floor of 2 x 2-inch gray-veined marble tile with a diamond-shaped insert. I loved it so much that I decided to use it for the fireplace surround too.

- Plenty of comfortable seating for friends was a priority in this renovation, so I started with my Lola sectional sofa—it tucks right into the enclosed porch at the front of the house. Since it will be exposed to strong sunlight, I covered it in an incredible, soft, chenille-like fabric in a very pale shade that won't show the effects of bleaching.

- For the channel-back sofa in the living area, I chose a gray antique velvet, and for the daybed, a cool, contemporary fabric in metallic tones of gray-blue. I used the same fabric on the backs of the upholstered dining chairs to tie the two spaces together.

- To soften the windows, I chose a beautiful linen damask in an ivory tone and paired it with sheers to diffuse the light and provide some privacy.

- New windows and lighting banish the dark and cramped feeling, and to make the most of that light, I bathed all the walls, ceiling, moldings, and cabinetry in the same creamy white tones. The soft, neutral envelope of color makes the whole space feel airy, modern, and fresh.

- In the new dining area, Carl and Tony can now seat as many as ten around a beautiful new solid-mahogany dining table with a hand-carved base. For everyday use, they can take out the three leaves and collapse the table down to a more intimate 44-inch length.

RIGHT: Enclosing the old porch added floor space and tons more light that streams in through big new windows that respect the house's age and character. A sectional with a chaise component fits snugly into this sunny nook and forms a secondary conversation area with the daybed.

4

FAMILY ROOMS AND GREAT ROOMS

WAY ABOVE PAR

CHALLENGE

Carrol and Paul are big-time golf enthusiasts with a home near their favorite golf club. They've updated the décor throughout the house except in the formal living room, which happens to be the largest space available for entertaining. They love having friends over to watch golf tournaments on TV, but the outdated furniture says "Victorian tea time" instead of "tee time," the ceiling bulges from an unfortunate leak, and a bed sheet pinned to the wall serves as a projection screen. I'm going to give them a mulligan—a do-over—to make this the ultimate family room for watching golf and entertaining.

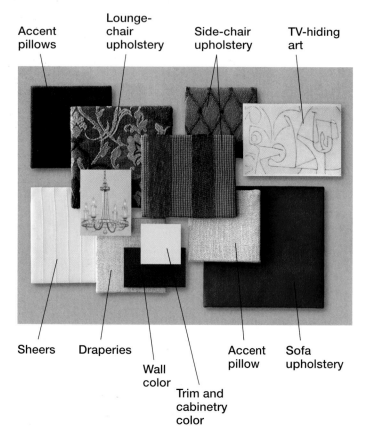

Accent pillows · Lounge-chair upholstery · Side-chair upholstery · TV-hiding art · Sheers · Draperies · Wall color · Trim and cabinetry color · Accent pillow · Sofa upholstery

BEFORE: This large formal room was drab and dated, with clunky recessed ceiling fixtures and anaglypta wallpaper everywhere. The furniture was too small for the space and too flowery and formal for Carrol and Paul's more casual lifestyle. And that bed-sheet-projection screen didn't add anything to the décor!

AFTER: Rich chocolate walls wrap the room in cozy warmth, and new bookcases flank the fireplace, giving it greater visual weight and presence. New sofas and chairs marry traditional elegance with casual everyday comfort and divide the room into zones for conversation and light meals. You'll never guess where the TV is!

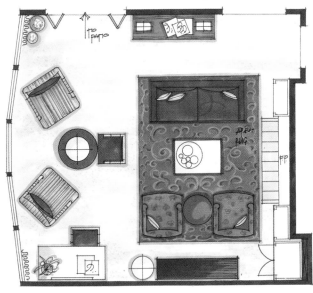

SOLUTION

- Before I could do anything else, I had to fix the ceiling. The anaglypta wallpaper and old ceiling came down, and new drywall went up, along with new, more modern recessed lighting all around the perimeter.

- To give the existing fireplace more visual presence, I flanked it with new floor-to-ceiling cabinetry. I used heavy glass for the top shelves so that light from the recessed fixtures could shine down through the glass to illuminate the objects on display. Mirror backing reflects the light back into the room and creates the illusion of greater depth and dimension on this entire wall.

- To replace Paul's bed-sheet projection screen, I put a big-screen TV on the wall adjacent to the fireplace. It hangs above a 34-inch-high console that holds all the media equipment. The coolest part is that it's hidden by a painting that rolls up out of sight when you press a button on the remote control.

- Lots of people to entertain means lots of places to sit. A big, comfy sofa placed at 90 degrees to the fireplace is perfectly positioned for viewing the new TV. A pair of low chairs faces the sofa over a coffee table for conversation, and the chairs won't block the TV when it's time to watch a tournament.

- Over in front of the windows, I created a secondary grouping that doubles as a spot for casual dining. A 30-inch-high table and French-style chairs offer a place to grab a snack or have drinks and enjoy the view of the backyard. The chairs are light enough that they can be pulled over in front of the TV when needed.

LEFT: A remote-controlled roller screen printed with abstract art retracts to reveal the big-screen television on the wall. The low-arm lounge chairs are only 36 inches tall, so they don't block the view of the television.

ABOVE: I painted the old mantel and doors a crisp white to match the new cabinetry and crown molding. Open shelves backed with mirror give the fireplace wall lots more depth and dimension, and the sparkly reflections help keep the chocolate-brown walls from being overwhelming. To ground the main seating group and bring in a little pattern, I layered a chocolate-brown rug over the existing wall-to-wall carpet.

ABOVE: A 30-inch-tall pedestal table anchors the secondary seating group. Surrounded by three inviting French-style chairs, it's a perfect spot for a snack or morning coffee. At the windows, a fresh, simple treatment of linen dummy panels and pinstriped sheers won't take away from the view. On the doors to the patio, a vinyl graphic with the look of etched glass provides a little privacy.

STYLE ELEMENTS

- Color is the key to creating cozy, inviting warmth in this room. I took my inspiration from the rug in the adjoining dining room: Its raspberry, cream, chocolate, and tan pattern suggested the scrumptious chocolate for the walls and succulent raspberry for the sofa.

- To balance the dark, enveloping chocolate walls, I contrasted them with creamy white cabinetry, trim, and ceilings. Dark walls can be intimidating, but remember that you'll be living with them as the background for furniture and accessories, which keep them from being overwhelming.

- Carrol and Paul wanted the room to be traditional in keeping with the rest of the house, but they also wanted it to be put-your-feet-up comfortable. To preserve a nice, open look, I chose a sofa with low arms, but the traditional detailing and slight camelback curve of the profile bring in the traditional elegance that Carrol likes. A solid-color sofa called for pattern on the chairs, which introduced beautiful color that I could use everywhere else.

- One entire wall of this room is windows that overlook lush woodlands. I framed the fabulous view with elegant, tailored dummy panels of crisp, creamy linen. Simple pinstripe sheers softly filter light but don't take away from the view. To hide the drapery hardware and the 14-foot-long bulkhead, I attached a valance made up of individual rectangular sections layered to create the look of kick pleats.

- The doors leading to the backyard had been covered with pocket sheers to filter light and provide privacy. For a more updated look, I replaced them with a frosted vinyl graphic applied to the glass. The Victorian design suits Carrol's traditional tastes and looks like etched glass.

- Modern recessed fixtures provide overall illumination and wash the walls with light. To bring more intimate lighting down into the room, I hung a sparkly chandelier over the small dining area and matching sconces above the fireplace. With a little bit of crystal and a classic design, they're timeless.

RIGHT: Overlapping panels of linen create the look of kick pleats. They're secured to the bulkhead with hook-and-loop tape and embellished with a covered button for a little extra sophistication. The chandelier's classic shape and sparkly crystals capture the look of traditional elegance that Carrol wanted.

CELEBRATION CENTRAL

CHALLENGE

Jyoti and Peter's 1980s suburban home is Celebration Central for their two large families. This multicultural, multigenerational family embraces a variety of religious traditions, and that means *lots* of holiday gatherings! Food is always a big part of the festivities, and the family room is right next to the kitchen, so that's where everyone ends up. Unfortunately, with its worn carpet, miles of dated mirrored walls, and ugly purple (yes, purple!) fireplace, the room is falling far short of festive and fabulous. Jyoti and Peter would love to have an elegant and welcoming space where they can keep the magic of the holidays alive all year long.

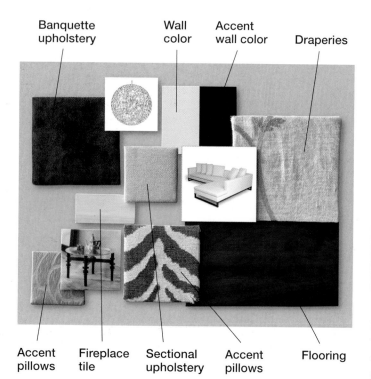

Banquette upholstery · Wall color · Accent wall color · Draperies

Accent pillows · Fireplace tile · Sectional upholstery · Accent pillows · Flooring

BEFORE: Mirror is great for expanding the sense of space, but you can overdo it. Plus, the fireplace sticks out like a sore thumb against all that reflective surface. Mismatched furniture circles around the worn carpeting, but there's not enough seating for big family gatherings.

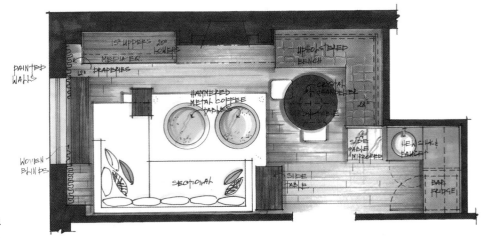

AFTER: Designed with festive gatherings in mind, the room now offers lots of seating, along with handy places to put food and drinks. A sleek, contemporary wall of limestone frames a functioning fireplace and defines a fresh, new feeling for the space.

SOLUTION

- Taking this room from drab to fab started with tearing out the hulking fireplace, removing the mirrored panels, and pulling up the old carpet. Then I put in a new, functioning fireplace surrounded by a wall of large-format limestone tile for a clean, contemporary look.

- Parties and carpeting add up to spills and stains, so in place of the carpet, I laid down a beautiful, practical, prefinished hardwood floor—easy to install, easy to clean, and perfect for a room that will see lots of eating and drinking!

- To pack maximum function into the space, I organized it into three zones that flow together seamlessly: a bar area, a party nook, and a comfortable and welcoming lounge area.

- I updated the bar area with a new configuration that opens to the family room (see page 175). It's much more functional with new stock cabinetry, a super-handy under-counter beverage fridge, a durable quartz countertop, and a big bar sink with faceted sides that catch the light.

- Adjoining the bar area, in the corner where the big free-standing TV had been, I built a cool L-shaped banquette with a table. With its high upholstered back and room for six, the banquette defines a cozy nook that's ideal for informal meals or a party.

- The new fireplace is the focal point of the lounge area. Beside it I built a media center, complete with a flat-panel TV and custom cabinetry to hide all the hardware and practical stuff.

- Opposite the fireplace and media center, a roomy L-shaped sectional sofa offers tons of comfy seating for Jyoti and Peter's family and friends. Two hammered-metal coffee tables can hold snacks and drinks.

LEFT: A new media center in espresso-stained wood incorporates the TV into the room's architecture so it doesn't dominate the space. Simple grommet-topped dummy panels frame the window for softness and some sparkle, and woven-wood blinds offer a little privacy.

ABOVE: An L-shaped banquette tucked into one corner of the room creates a cozy nook for meals and gatherings. The charcoal velvet upholstery is an easy-to-clean polyester that hides spills and stains. Above the banquette, a strip of mirror catches the light from that spectacular crystal-ball chandelier and reflects it back into the room. Clad in smooth, 12 x 24-inch limestone tiles, the fireplace column sets a contemporary mood that contrasts with the more traditional look of the banquette's tufted back.

STYLE ELEMENTS

- Light is a theme in holiday celebrations of all religious traditions, and that became the common thread in my choices for lighting, fabrics, finishes, and colors. Lots of recessed ceiling fixtures on dimmer switches provide even, overall illumination, but the real "wow" factor comes from a spectacular crystal-ball chandelier. Bling, bling, bling! This fixture captures what the space is all about—it reminds me of the ball that drops on New Year's Eve, and I love the way the light hits it and refracts through it. It's perfect for a room that's all about light and celebration.

- Light also comes into play with the fabrics. For the banquette, I chose an inky charcoal fabric with a sparkly thread woven through it. Accent pillows in shimmery, satiny fabrics catch the light, and at the windows, dummy panels in a neutral linen twinkle with a swirly scroll pattern in metallic pewter.

- For the fireplace, I chose a beautiful, sleek limestone tile with cool tones of white, gray, and buff in a strié finish. A creamy mushroom-colored grout blends in with the tile so the overall impact on the room is light and clean.

- The creamy tones of the limestone tiles inspired the stone-colored upholstery for the sectional on the opposite wall.

- To contrast with the sectional and add depth to the room, I painted the wall behind it midnight blue to relate to the charcoal fabric on the banquette. The rest of the walls are a light, neutral tone to blend with the tiles around the fireplace.

- A dark, rich walnut tone for the floor gives the room a feeling of luxury and sophistication. Wood in a similar espresso-brown tone trims the banquette and makes up the media cabinet.

- I took a lot of mirror out of this room, but I put just a little back in, above the media center and the banquette, to reflect light and add to the ambience of sparkle and shine.

LEFT: The clean, contemporary lines and stone color of the fireplace meet their match on the opposite wall, where a long, L-shaped sectional defines the lounging zone of the family room. I accented this wall with dark midnight-blue paint to speak back to the night-sky color of the banquette and give the room more depth.

LEFT: Family photos turn into seasonal decorations with the help of self-adhesive magnetic sheets. Just attach the holiday photo to the magnetic sheet and apply it over the glass of the framed photos.

BELOW: This super-cool bar sink has a faceted interior that catches the light and adds to the room's sparkly ambience. With a black quartz countertop, the bar area can serve as a satellite mini-kitchen for simple food prep as well as buffet service.

RIGHT: I just love this crystal-ball chandelier! It takes lighting to a whole new level. The reconfigured bar area is now more functional, with an under-counter beverage refrigerator as well as a sink and serving surface. A pair of stools round out the seating in the banquette nook and can move elsewhere as needed.

MULTIFUNCTIONAL MEETS MAXI-COMFORTABLE

CHALLENGE

Peter and Anna have nearly finished a year-long, full-scale renovation, but they still have to tackle the great room, and they're fresh out of energy and ideas. This is supposed to be their "wowee" room for entertaining—a multifunctional space that they can enjoy with their baby daughter or with a crowd. Peter is a former national team water polo player and still plays for fun, so having his teammates over is definitely on the agenda. Right now, however, the room is big, empty, and underfurnished, with no color or style. I'm ready to dive in and turn it into a space that really makes a splash!

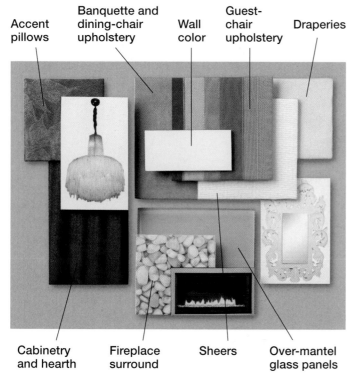

Accent pillows · Banquette and dining-chair upholstery · Wall color · Guest-chair upholstery · Draperies

Cabinetry and hearth · Fireplace surround · Sheers · Over-mantel glass panels

BEFORE: The new great room was almost finished, with primed walls awaiting a color choice. Peter and Anna wanted it to be a modern, hip, multifunctional space that is also cozy and inviting, but they didn't know how to get there.

AFTER: Two steps up from the kitchen, this great room really *is* great! Two fabulous feature walls anchor two different zones, one for dining and one for conversation and watching TV.

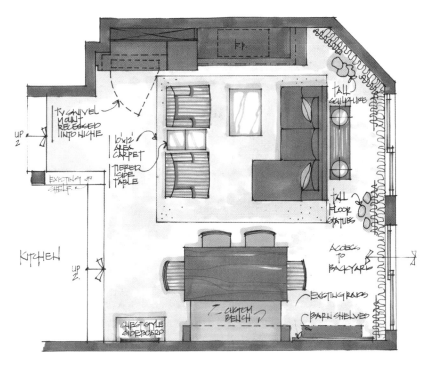

ABOVE: With the wall of cabinetry tucked into the corner nearest the room's entrance, I could make the fireplace the focal point of the living area. I had to build out the wall to contain the exhaust pipe and gas insert. Then I finished the expanse above the firebox with glass panels back-painted a watery blue-gray. A scrumptious faux sheepskin rug anchors the seating.

SOLUTION

- To tame this big space, I started by dividing it into a dining area on one side, easily accessible from the kitchen, and a living area on the opposite side. I took advantage of the bulkhead and some funny jogs on one wall to build in a bank of cabinetry and add a fireplace.

- Peter would like to watch sports with his buddies in here, but Anna doesn't want the TV to dominate, so I tucked the big flat-panel TV into a wall of custom-built cabinetry and mounted it on a swivel. When they want to watch a show, they simply pull the TV forward and angle it toward the lounge area.

- The only construction needed was to put in a fireplace. That required framing and drywalling, running a gas line, installing an exhaust pipe, and putting in a firebox to hold the gas insert. Instead of faux logs, the fireplace features marble stones for the chic, modern look the couple wanted.

- In front of the fireplace I positioned a super-cushy sectional with a chaise component and a couple of my Maxine guest chairs.

- Usually I do only one feature wall, but this room was screaming for drama, so I gave it two— one with the fireplace and gorgeous cabinetry and one on the opposite wall, where a super-sized banquette adds drama to dinner.

ABOVE: The television pulls out of its niche and swivels toward the sectional when Peter and Anna want to watch TV. Otherwise, it tucks discreetly back into the cabinetry.

- The room already had a ton of recessed fixtures in the ceiling, so I just added recessed puck lights in the bulkhead of the banquette and hung an incredible, super-elegant crystal chandelier over the dining table. Nothing says "Dining room here" like a fabulous chandelier!

STYLE ELEMENTS

- The great room is completely open to the kitchen, which has a cherry-toned island and built-in desk, so I used the same wood for the new cabinetry, banquette, and hearth in the great room. It's important to have finishes speak to each other in a big, open-concept space so there's flow and unity throughout.

- Peter's water polo career inspired the color scheme and the fireplace treatment. To make the fireplace a show-stopping focal point for the room, I clad the wall above the firebox with ultramodern glass panels. By itself, glass is greenish, so I painted the back of the panels a cool gray hue before installing them. The result is a watery look reminiscent of pool water.

- To frame the firebox, I found a fabulous tile made up of tumbled river rock embedded in a resin-epoxy binder. Cutting the tiles is tricky and requires a wet saw, but with smooth cuts and a tight, groutless installation, the result is spectacular—seamless, modern, yet natural.

- To upholster the Maxine guest chairs, I found a crisp cotton stripe with brown that picks up on the cherry cabinetry and watery green-blue stripes that inspired accent pillows and the banquette upholstery. A caramel-colored sofa sectional speaks to the brown in the stripe as well as to the floor color.

- A great dining area needs great seating. My Diana chairs are super-comfy for long dinners and conversation around a beautiful, modern dining table.

- Windows of different heights took up one whole wall at the end of the room. I unified them with a combination of window treatments—polyester sheers with a little stripe to filter light and soft drapery panels in a cream microfiber to frame them. The sheers, topped with single pleats, don't detract from the beautiful views or abundant light.

- Peter and Anna couldn't decide on a color for the walls, so I chose a clean, warm white that picks up on the kitchen cabinetry and makes a subtle, neutral backdrop for the furnishings.

- A faux sheepskin rug unifies the living area and defines a path from the kitchen to the windows at the end of the room.

LEFT: There's just nothing like a chandelier to add splashy drama to a space! This one, with its hundreds of strands of beads dangling in concentric circles, is contemporary, showy, and super-fun.

BELOW: A super-sized banquette backed with button-tufted panels says, "Sit down, relax, enjoy!" Puck lights installed in the top of the unit play up the texture of the tufting. Upholstered dining chairs with a sculpted profile nod to traditional style, but their straight legs and simple shapes blend well with the clean lines of the modern table.

LOFT LIVING

A PLACE TO CALL HOME

CHALLENGE

Anurita traded in her job as a journalist to work as an advocate for HIV patients and children in Africa. Her work keeps her away from home and living in hotel rooms for months at a time, so when she comes back to her small downtown loft, she'd like it to be a comfortable, welcoming place to unwind. The space has terrific bones—hardwood floors, exposed brick and ductwork, big windows, and wonderful high ceilings. What it's lacking is furniture, style, and that indefinable something that makes a space feel like home—and that's where I come in.

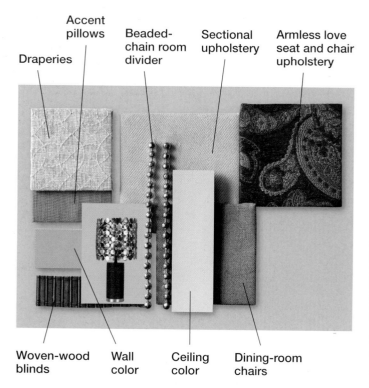

Accent pillows
Draperies
Beaded-chain room divider
Sectional upholstery
Armless love seat and chair upholstery
Woven-wood blinds
Wall color
Ceiling color
Dining-room chairs

BEFORE: Anurita's compact urban loft had great potential but very little in the way of furniture or personality. Her dining table doubled as her home office, and the only place to sit was on the floor.

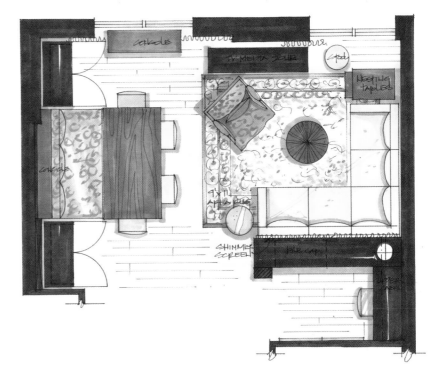

AFTER: Color, furniture, and window treatments transformed a bare-bones space into a comfortable, casual, multifunctional room where Anurita can relax, work, and even host international guests who come to visit.

SOLUTION

- The loft was in great shape structurally, so the big challenge was how to organize the space and put every square inch to work. I relocated the office to one corner and divided it from the living area with a new 9-foot-long console that aligns with the support column. (It's not easy to get a 9-foot-long console up the stairs to the fifth floor!) A floating wall cabinet keeps work stuff tucked out of sight, and a custom-built computer desk provides plenty of space for her laptop, books, and papers.

- Anurita loves the exposed brick, but I'm going to cover it—sort of. Oversized custom cabinetry enhances the soaring height of the loft ceiling and provides architectural interest, along with much-needed storage and display space. I left the shelves open to let the exposed brick show through (see page 188).

- In between the cabinets I inserted a long display shelf that doubles as a console table for upholstered seating that tucks in between the cabinets. An armless love seat and matching chair fit together snugly in the niche and provide super-comfy, space-saving seating for the dining area. A couple of skirted Parsons chairs and a pair of upholstered dining chairs surround Anurita's dining table and can be pulled over to the living area when she entertains.

- For the living area, I found the perfect solution: a big, L-shaped sectional that includes a built-in sleeper sofa with an inflatable mattress. Now the living room can double as a guest room when friends from overseas come to visit.

- The beautiful warehouse-style windows are among the loft's best features, but with all the hard surfaces, the windows needed a little softening to make this space feel more inviting. I hung gorgeous, floor-length linen panels to frame the windows. Woven-wood blinds with blackout lining provide light control, so guests can sleep past daybreak if they want to!

- The loft had plenty of junction boxes but no lighting, so I added a track of positionable halogen lights, dropping the track down 18 inches from the ceiling to clear the ductwork.

ABOVE: Zoning organizes the loft's main room into a dining area, a living area, and an office nook. (The kitchen is separated from the main room by a peninsula that doubles as a counter for casual dining.) New cabinetry puts the vertical space to work in the office and dining areas.

ABOVE: Soaring cabinetry in a rich, dark stain that matches the table anchors the dining area. I like a mix of closed and open storage in units like these for both aesthetic and practical reasons: The closed section visually weights the piece so it looks stable and solid, and the doors keep messy clutter out of sight. Open shelves above show off Anurita's collection of African art, with the rugged brick as a backdrop.

STYLE ELEMENTS

- Anurita loves her wooden dining table, so I used a similar dark stain for the console and all the new cabinetry. The dark espresso-brown finish also complements the brick.

- Only one of the three main walls was not brick, so I painted it a cool blue-gray that relates to the brick and balances its warm tones.

- That painted wall needed something distinctive. Since Anurita is a journalist, what could be more appropriate than a wall of words—specifically, a wall of her favorite inspirational quotes? I had quotations printed on vinyl transfer material in metallic inks and then rubbed them onto the wall. I love the way the treatment reads as wallpaper, but a very personal wallpaper.

- To give the loft an eclectic, layered-over-time look, I chose a mix of contemporary and traditional furnishings and fabrics. For the armless love seat and chair in the dining area, I found a luscious chenille-like paisley that's the perfect foil for all of the warm colors happening in the space. An upholstered armchair in the living area wears a large-scale, gold-and-cream pattern that brings in more traditional style. With all this pattern, I kept the contemporary sectional solid and neutral, with chic white herringbone upholstery. Solid blue and cream fabrics cover the dining room chairs.

- Over the dining table, a long light fixture with three bulbs hangs 60 inches above the floor and spreads light evenly along the table. I added a diffuser, which just rests on the inside edge of the shade, to prevent glare.

- Creamy linen draperies speak to the neutral color of the sectional but have a fun little embroidered detail that adds interest and texture. To tie the draperies in with the brick, I added a deep band of terra-cotta-colored strié along the bottom edge.

- The console divides the office physically from the living area. To screen the office nook visually, I installed a super-cool curtain of metal beads. They hang from a track mounted on the ceiling and bring in a touch of industrial bling.

RIGHT: Anurita's favorite inspirational quotes, printed in metallic gold, bronze, and silver inks, turn the painted wall into a personal statement. Vinyl transfer graphics make the process pretty easy—the hardest part is making sure each line of type is level and straight. (A laser level helps here!) The curtain of metallic beads shimmers in the light of ceiling-mounted halogen tracks and adds a bit of industrial-style sparkle to the room.

LEFT: Filing cabinets tuck under the custom-built console, which also provides lots of tabletop surface for working. Wall-hung storage above the custom-built computer desk keeps all of Anurita's office stuff tidy and organized.

OPPOSITE: To give the loft that lived-in, I'm-finally-at-home feeling, I mixed traditional, primitive, and contemporary furnishings. A French-style bergère upholstered in a large-scale pattern introduces a little traditional style, in contrast with the simple lines of a farmhouse table. An open side table resembles an African drum and has a gold finish that picks up on the French chair's upholstery.

LOFTY IDEAS

CHALLENGE

Rocco bought a sixth-floor penthouse condo and then promptly left for Australia for a volleyball tournament. That vacation turned into six years of work and play. Now he's back, but the big box he calls home isn't screaming "hip, cool, urban loft"—it's just screaming! The ceilings are not only incredibly high, but they're also multilevel. The fireplace doesn't work, the kitchen is outdated, and the décor doesn't reflect his style at all. He's asked me for an assist, and I just can't say no to a fellow volleyball player!

Accent wall and kitchen cabinet color

Cabinetry

Wall and ceiling color

Upper-kitchen cabinet color

Tile backsplash

BEFORE: The condo had the soaring ceilings, huge windows, and great views that everyone loves about a loft, but the color scheme belonged to the 1980s and the fireplace didn't work. The plants were left by a tenant. The mismatched chairs and plastic storage tubs? They've got to go too!

AFTER: Clean white ceilings and walls unify the space, and accent walls in deep teal pick up the color of the updated kitchen cabinets. In place of the old angled fireplace wall, a new boxlike wall for the TV marks the division between the living area and the office. The new placement, aligned with the exterior wall, actually makes the space feel larger by opening up sight lines from the front of the condo to the back.

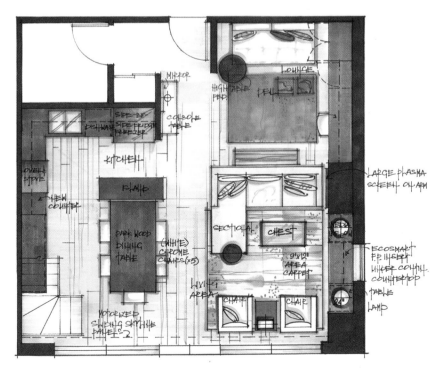

ABOVE: A big L-shaped sectional anchors the living area and faces the condo's real focal point: a stunning view of the city. I tucked a clean-burning ethanol fireplace into the niche on the side wall for ambience as well as a little warmth. Track-mounted translucent panels pull easily across the windows on both levels to provide privacy and diffuse daylight.

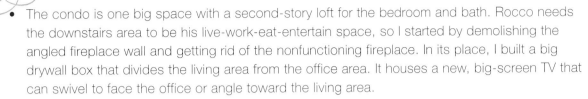

SOLUTION

- The condo is one big space with a second-story loft for the bedroom and bath. Rocco needs the downstairs area to be his live-work-eat-entertain space, so I started by demolishing the angled fireplace wall and getting rid of the nonfunctioning fireplace. In its place, I built a big drywall box that divides the living area from the office area. It houses a new, big-screen TV that can swivel to face the office or angle toward the living area.

- I couldn't put in a gas fireplace, so I did the next best thing and installed a clean-burning ethanol-fueled fireplace that needs no venting. It's the centerpiece of a new bank of cabinetry that fits under the side window.

- On the other side of the new TV wall, I continued the custom-built cabinetry with a long desk, shelves, and storage cabinets for Rocco's office. He also wants to be able to accommodate overnight guests, so I brought in a daybed sofa with an ingenious design: You pull it away from the wall a little and flip up the backrest, and voilà! It's a twin bed ready for sheets and pillows.

- The L-shaped kitchen just needed a facelift—but a major one. I gave it a whole new look with paint, new countertops, and a new backsplash. I also made it a lot more functional by extending the cabinets to the ceiling and adding two new base cabinets to extend the usable storage space under the stairs.

- To give Rocco a place to feed his friends, I positioned a table and chairs perpendicular to the kitchen island.

- With 19-foot ceilings and that wall of windows, the condo could get really hot and stuffy in the summer, especially up in the bedroom. To help with air circulation, I installed two incredible fans—each one has two heads with really big wooden blades. They're stunning! But no more indoor volleyball.

- I deep-sixed the existing bulky sheers, which didn't provide privacy and were difficult to pull across the windows. In their place, I installed beautiful translucent panels that slide on a track. You can order them in a variety of colors, patterns, and light-blocking strengths. I chose a level two, which softens and diffuses the light but doesn't obscure the view.

RIGHT: A column of walnut cabinetry balances the TV wall and provides tons of storage for Rocco's new office. The office sofa turns into a twin bed if any of Rocco's pals from Australia comes to visit. A sleek steel-and-wood console table backs up to the sectional sofa and can double as an office work surface if needed.

STYLE ELEMENTS

- Giving the condo a cool, hip, urban look to match Rocco's personality started with the kitchen. I replaced the old backsplash with sleek, linear glass tiles in dark-to-light tones of light green to dark blue-green. The tiles gave me the key to the color scheme for the rest of the space.

- A two-tone paint job updated the kitchen cabinets: a smoky teal on the base cabinets contrasts with the light floor, and oyster-white refreshes the upper cabinets. New glass and pewter knobs for the cabinetry pick up on the backsplash and enhance the modern look.

- For the counters, I chose a shiny black quartz to flow into the existing appliances.

- I painted the old industrial-concrete ceilings white to give the condo a clean, modern look and to blend the new lighting conduit and fixtures into the background. Using the same hue on the walls and stair unifies the whole space. To add interest and to accent the functional zones, I painted the TV wall and one office wall with the same smoky teal as the base cabinets in the kitchen.

- To balance all of the cool, neutral color, I chose a beautiful mid-tone walnut for the custom cabinetry. It looks gorgeous against the walls and adds just the right touch of warmth.

- A cool, hip, funky loft means cool, hip, funky furniture: An armless sectional keeps the look open, and its exposed stainless-steel legs give it a contemporary, industrial vibe. The dark gray upholstery speaks back to the quartz counters in the kitchen.

- Lighting helps focus attention on the new finishes. A xenon fixture under the kitchen cabinets highlights the glass tile and quartz countertop. Puck lights under the office shelves illuminate the desk, and strips of track lights provide general illumination throughout.

RIGHT: The existing cabinets had modern slab-front doors and drawers but needed a little facelift. Fresh paint in two contrasting colors and new pewter-and-glass hardware gave them an updated look.

BELOW: Two new base cabinets tucked under the stairs turn wasted space into functional storage with more countertop for food prep. I also took the wall cabinets all the way up to the ceiling to expand the tiny kitchen's storage capabilities. A sleek, modern table snugs up against the island to give Rocco a much-needed dining area.

6 BASEMENTS (YES, BASEMENTS!)

THE CURE FOR DISCO FEVER

CHALLENGE

Lori bought her childhood home from her parents and looks forward to living there for years to come. The basement her father designed and finished in the 1970s was once a hip and happenin' place, but now it just feels dark and dated. And believe me, it's the 1970s at its finest, with wood shingles, dropped acoustical-tile ceilings, stucco walls, and barn-board paneling and beams. All it's missing is the disco ball and a fondue set. Lori likes the copper-hooded fireplace, but she wants to trade the dark and gloomy dungeon feel for a lighter, brighter look that will make the room a comfortable, elegant place to relax, entertain, and watch movies.

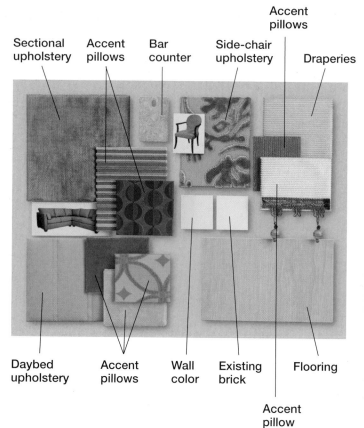

Sectional upholstery · Accent pillows · Bar counter · Side-chair upholstery · Accent pillows · Draperies · Daybed upholstery · Accent pillows · Wall color · Existing brick · Accent pillow · Flooring

BEFORE: Lori's basement was a cornucopia of 1970s building materials, including ebony-stained barn wood, concrete floors, an acoustical-tile ceiling, and orange-and-brown carpeting. With no natural light and a hodgepodge of cast-off furniture, the basement felt drab and dated.

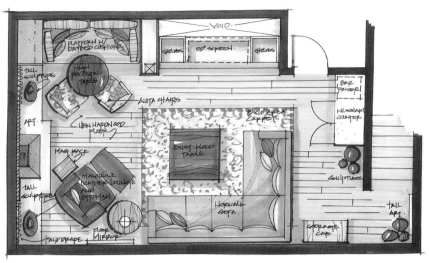

AFTER: All those old 1970s materials are still there, but they're totally transformed with paint. The copper hood over the fireplace shows up better than ever, framed by luminous, creamy white brick and draperies that create the illusion of windows. A new wall of cabinetry houses a media center, storage, and a reading nook.

SOLUTION

- I used an existing support post to define two zones, one for reading beside the fireplace and one for conversation and watching TV. I encased the support post and an attached partial wall in a medium-density fiberboard (MDF) box that divides the reading nook from the media center nook.

- My secret weapon for bringing this space out of the 1970s—and doing it on a budget—was paint. But because all the wood had been stained nearly black, everything had to be primed first with a stain-blocking primer. Then I applied a beautiful, warm antique white to absolutely every surface except the floor and the hearth. Brick, beams, wainscoting, walls, acoustical tiles, and frames all underwent a total transformation, replacing the dark dungeon with a light, bright shell.

- To update the floor, I put down new laminate flooring right over the old concrete floors. It was a two-step process: First, a plasticized foam lining was rolled out over the concrete to provide a vapor barrier and help muffle sound. Then laminate planks were laid on top, clicking together for a nearly seamless look. The planks are thin so they don't diminish the height of the room—an important consideration in a basement with a low ceiling.

- Lori loved the fireplace and wanted it to be a focal point, so I played up the good bits—the copper hood—and hid the not-so-good bits—the brick and barn board—with paint and fabric. To mask the barn-board walls flanking the fireplace, I hung simple grommet-topped draperies over them. Not only do they create the illusion of windows, but one also hides the electrical panel.

- For the media center, I designed custom-built cabinetry that tucks snugly into one nook and showcases a big flat-panel TV with open shelves on each side and drawers for storage below. For the reading nook, I designed a twin-sized platform bed with bookshelves at one end.

- On the back wall of the basement, I installed a floating shelf and a bar counter. A beverage fridge and a wheeled cart tucked underneath the counter will save Lori and her husband the trouble of running upstairs for snacks or drinks on movie nights (see page 205).

- The one redeeming feature of the basement, from the electrical point of view, was the dropped ceiling. The removable tiles made it easy to install lots of low-voltage recessed halogen fixtures that wash the walls with light and direct attention away from the ceiling. Recessed fixtures in the bulkhead above the TV and reading nook add sparkly accent lighting. Wall sconces shed cozy light over the daybed.

RIGHT: The custom-built entertainment center tucks snugly into the niche created by an encased support post on one side and the bulkhead above. I used budget-friendly MDF to build the cabinetry and gave it a high-end look by trimming the edges of the shelves with real wood. The horizontal surfaces of the shelves and the back of the entire unit are painted to match the wood stain.

BELOW: Antique-white paint unifies all the disparate materials—wood shingles, brick, barn board, and stucco. Panels of fabric continue the envelope of color but add dimension and softness—and create the illusion that the subterranean room has windows. I turned the existing bulkhead into an advantage and created a reading nook at this end of the room. The bookshelves rest on a platform that's high enough to serve as an armrest, foot board, or side table.

BELOW: Paint and new lighting banished the old dungeon feeling, and new furniture updates the room with casual elegance. I chose an L-shaped sectional with clean, modern lines for the main seating. Button-tufted back cushions, nailhead trim, and soft velvet upholstery give it a little bit of a traditional feel to blend with the classic leather club chair. I cut down the legs of Lori's old table so it could serve as a coffee table in her new digs.

STYLE ELEMENTS

- Solid wood is beautiful, but it's expensive. To keep this redo on budget, I built the cabinetry out of inexpensive MDF and painted it to blend in with the walls. For an elegant touch, I trimmed the front edges of the shelves with hardwood and painted the horizontal surfaces to match. You get the high-end look and durability of solid wood without the expense. Groovy!

- The laminate flooring is also a high-style budget-stretcher. Wood laminate gives the appearance of real wood at a fraction of the cost, and the natural maple finish I chose helps make the whole basement feel fresh and light.

- I replaced all of Lori's old hand-me-down furniture with a collection of modern and traditional pieces. A big, beautiful sectional with clean, modern lines anchors the TV-watching zone. In the reading zone, a leather club chair keeps the daybed company next to the fireplace. A pedestal table and an occasional chair pull up to the daybed so Lori and her husband can use this area for games or snacks.

- For comfort and warmth, I chose an eclectic mix of traditional and contemporary fabrics in wonderful, touchable textures. The daybed mattress is upholstered in a creamy quilted fabric that's very tactile. The sectional wears a platinum-blue velvet that contrasts with the warmth of the copper hood on the fireplace. Accent pillows in a shimmery copper-toned geometric, a modern damask, and stripes add more pattern to break up the solid expanses of the sectional and the daybed.

- The only item besides the fireplace that Lori wanted to keep was a table her brother had built for her. I cut down the legs so it could serve as a coffee table in the new space.

ABOVE: Even though its disco days are long gone, the basement will still be a place for entertaining family and friends. I added a beverage fridge and bar counter to keep drinks handy and provide plenty of space for serving snacks.

PARTY PERFECT

CHALLENGE

Steve is a fabulous party and event planner who loves to entertain family and friends in his home. The problem is that the best party space is a dated 1960s basement that is frankly an embarrassment. It's shabby but not chic, with bland wood paneling, a brittle vinyl floor, multiple pieced-together carpets, and hand-me-down furniture. The bar is covered with faux-wood peel-and-stick paper (eek!), and the corner brick fireplace is stained with soot. This sad space needs a major makeover to become a gathering space worthy of Steve's party-planning talents!

BEFORE: The 1960s live on in Steve's basement, with its pressed-wood paneling, old tile ceiling, worn-out "carpettes," and cracking vinyl flooring. The hand-me-down furniture has seen better days, and the bar is actually covered with faux-wood paper.

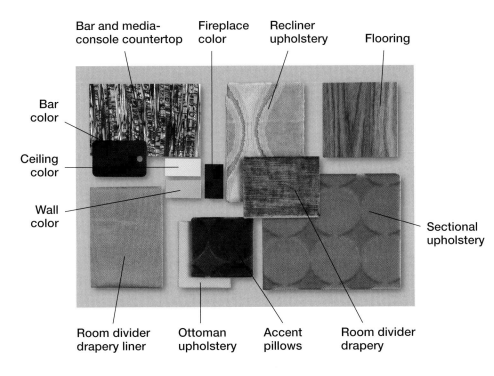

Bar and media-console countertop

Fireplace color

Recliner upholstery

Flooring

Bar color

Ceiling color

Wall color

Sectional upholstery

Room divider drapery liner

Ottoman upholstery

Accent pillows

Room divider drapery

AFTER: It's amazing what you can do with a little paint—or a lot of it, in this case. Paint transformed the walls, ceiling, fireplace, and bar, while new vinyl flooring added the warm, natural look of wood without the cost. Now the room is ready for a party of 2 or 20—or even more!

SOLUTION

- The room was outdated from floor to ceiling, but gallons of paint whipped it into shape without breaking the budget. Primer and paint revived the old ceiling tiles, transformed the paneling, and gave a whole new look to the bar.

- Steve likes to use the wood-burning fireplace, but soot was a little bit of a problem. I painted the brick to match the soot, and problem solved! I covered the puny concrete mantel with a new wood mantel painted to match the brick. The new mantel fits right over the old one and stretches across the entire corner, giving the fireplace more presence and panache.

- The bar came with the house, but it was really just a big box with no style. I ripped off the faux-wood peel-and-stick paper and completely restyled the bar with paint and one of the coolest new flooring materials I've seen.

- The old carpet scraps and vinyl flooring were carted out to the dumpster and replaced with vinyl wood flooring. This material is perfect for a party room—it's flexible, resilient, durable, affordable, and easy to maintain. And it's good for below-grade installations where dampness or flooding might be a problem.

- Steve loves his media equipment, but his old TV stand left a labyrinth of wires exposed in a tangled mess. I tidied it up with a long custom-built media wall that includes a base piece for organizing all the components—woofers, tweeters, meowers, and whatever else he needs!

- All the furniture had been handed down numerous times, and this was the end of the line. I replaced everything except the recliner, which came from Steve's grandfather. It got a new lease on life with new upholstery. A huge new sectional seats tons of people, and a couple of comfy, multifunctional upholstered benches double as seating or tables.

- There was practically no lighting in the room, so I brought in light with sconces, track lighting, and funky pendants.

- Steve needed a small home office down here, but he didn't want it to interfere with the party spirit. I screened the back corner of the room with some gorgeous metallic draperies to hide his desk and office chair and serve as a beautiful backdrop for the bar.

RIGHT: A new bulkhead above the bar hides the wiring for funky Sputnik-inspired pendants. At the back of the room, I installed ceiling-mounted draperies to divide the party area from Steve's home office.

ABOVE: The fireplace deserves to be a focal point now, thanks to a coat of black paint and a new wood mantel that fits right over the old concrete one. The new mantel is longer, extending onto the angled walls on either side, so it's in better proportion to the hearth. On the wall above, frosted glass cylinders on rectangular stainless-steel plates provide intimate accent lighting and a sleek, modern look.

STYLE ELEMENTS

- My inspiration for colors in this room came from a gorgeous vinyl floor tile that was just too fabulous to put on the floor. Instead, I used it to cover the top of the bar and the media-center counter. It has a beautiful iridescent blue and charcoal gray ribbon-like pattern and a mother-of-pearl finish. The tiles are simply glued in place to a new board that I laid over the top of the old bar. I painted the base of the bar and the media center glossy charcoal gray to speak back to the fireplace color.

- Pulling the iridescent blue from the vinyl tile, I painted all of the walls a soft, icy blue and freshened the ceiling with cool white.

- To balance the cool walls, I chose a warm champagne-gold chenille mohair for the new sectional. The geometric print adds subtle, modern pattern, as does the two-toned champagne-colored velvet I chose for the old recliner.

- For the curtain that separates the office from the party space, I combined two luscious, silky, gray metallic fabrics and hung them with grommets on a simple rod.

- Lighting helps modernize the space too. Over the fireplace I installed a pair of very contemporary sconces for intimate mood lighting. Above the bar area, I added a bulkhead to accommodate junction boxes for three glass Sputnik pendants that bring in a funky retro look. A line of new halogen track lights down the center of the room can be positioned to lighten dark corners.

BELOW: A cool new media console consists of two units: one a standard table with open storage and one a floating box with cubbies. A single countertop unites them. I designed the console to allow room for an upholstered bench to slide underneath.

OPPOSITE: Charcoal-gray paint and a new countertop give the old bar sophisticated new style. The vinyl tiles that cover the countertop are intended for use on the floor, but I thought they were so gorgeous that I wanted to bring them higher, where you could really see the beautiful striated pattern and pearlescent finish. The tiles are simply glued in place on the countertop, with little strips glued to the edges for a finished look.

GLITZY, GLITTERY, AND GLAM-FABULOUS

CHALLENGE

Michelle and Ruel are a cosmopolitan couple whose lives suddenly turned upside down when the birth of their first child was soon followed by the arrival of twins! The couple traded their cool city loft for a house in the 'burbs, but they've been too busy with changing diapers and 3 a.m. feedings to think about giving the place their own sense of style. The basement is the biggest room in the house, so it's the perfect space for entertaining friends, but they also want to share it with the kids. They've asked me to create a room that's gorgeous and glitzy for adults but also kid-friendly.

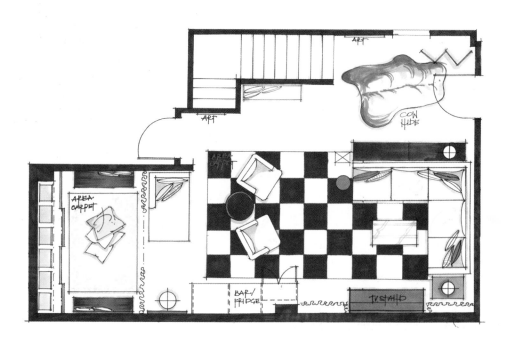

BEFORE: The basement was just a big, bland box with industrial wall-to-wall carpeting and lots of toys. A row of builder's-grade ceiling fixtures provided the only light.

AFTER: Beige and bland gave way to glitter and glam with a "Bollywood in the basement" makeover that reflects the couple's Indian and Chinese backgrounds. Beautiful paisley patterns and metallic gold finishes reference Michelle's traditional saris in a contemporary way. Zones organize the long space by function, with an emphasis on grownup entertaining in the media and lounge zones.

SOLUTION

- The basement was a clean, suburban slate and needed no renovating, so I started by dividing the space into three zones based on function: a TV zone with a media console and lots of seating; a lounge zone with a long bar counter, storage center, and energy-saving under-counter bar fridge; and a kids' play area with toy storage at the back (see pages 216 and 217).

- The room didn't need a lot of cabinetry, so I chose budget-friendly ready-to-assemble pieces for the media console and dry-bar area. To give the bar a high-style look without the price tag, I replaced the doors and drawer fronts, installed a custom-cut laminate countertop, and swapped out the original hardware for something more stylish.

- The room's one tiny window, located near the ceiling, was more like a fresh-air vent, so I covered it with a lavish window treatment of silk and velvet. A matching treatment on the other side of the TV console provides balance and creates the illusion of another window.

- A closet with mirrored doors filled the back wall of the kids' zone and was perfect for toy storage. I kept the mirrored doors but dressed them up with a vinyl transfer of a black chandelier design. I also used a little trick I learned from my mom: "out of sight, out of mind." Curtains pull across on a ceiling track, so when company comes, the clutter disappears (see page 216).

- When you have to stick to a budget, the easiest way to transform a space is with lighting. For $100 or less you can install track lights with energy-saving low-voltage bulbs. They can be positioned to highlight wallpaper, art, or a special feature, drawing attention to a focal point or creating a sense of drama.

LEFT: The big-screen TV disappears against the ebony console, which balances the black paisley wallpaper on the adjacent wall. Gold velvet over-draperies paired with luscious white silk curtains frame the console and add softness and dimension to the wall.

ABOVE: A fabulous feature wall covered in black and gold paisley anchors the TV zone and is the first thing you see when you come downstairs. Slipper chairs dressed in cream upholstery with an oversized paisley in metallic gold threads bring in the glitz and glam Michelle and Ruel wanted.

BELOW: The dry bar and chaise stake out the lounge zone, while the back of the room belongs to the kids. I kept the sliding mirrored doors on the big closet but gave them a major style facelift with vinyl graphic transfers of black chandeliers. If Michelle and Ruel want to hide the toy clutter fast, all they have to do is pull the draperies closed.

OPPOSITE: An energy-saving under-counter fridge keeps beverages and snacks handy. It's flanked by ready-to-assemble cabinets that look more expensive than they are thanks to ebony-stained doors and drawers and sparkly stainless-steel hardware.

STYLE ELEMENTS

- Ruel is Indian and Michelle is Indian and Chinese, and they wanted the space to reflect their backgrounds. An incredible sari of Michelle's kicked everything off—its sheer white fabric with a gold thread inspired the whole idea of metallics, sparkle, and bling.

- A large-scale paisley wallpaper with a metallic gold pattern on a black background sets the stage. It's the first thing you see as you come down the stairs, and it immediately says "exotic, exciting, grownup space!" Before putting up the paper, I painted the wall gray-blue, so if the paper shrinks a little, it won't be noticeable.

- For the lounge wall, I chose grass-cloth wallpaper with a gold metallic backing. It's sparkly and adds texture but doesn't detract from the paisley feature wall. I painted the remaining walls and support column a warm, goldish tone that picks up on the grass cloth.

- The large ebony console for the TV speaks to the black background of the paisley wallpaper, as do the ebony door and drawer fronts I used to upgrade the dry-bar cabinetry.

- For the bar countertop, I chose gold laminate and had it custom-cut to fit around the ductwork—there's gold in them thar counters! Sparkly custom pulls pick up on the stainless steel of the bar fridge and the brackets and shelves on the wall above.

- Super-comfy, space-saving furniture provides lots of seating for Michelle and Ruel's city friends. A huge sectional covered in a creamy fabric with a little gold fleck anchors the TV zone. Two slipper chairs in an overscaled cream-and-gold paisley pair up to frame the conversation area. In the lounge area, a big, plump chaise offers more seating.

- On either side of the TV console, I hung floor-length white silk draperies from rods installed on the ceiling. Over-draperies of luscious gold velvet add more fullness and richness.

- To break up the expanse of wall-to-wall carpeting, I laid a checkerboard of black and white carpet tiles right over the carpeting.

- Behind the sectional, an ebony bookcase offers super-practical storage.

OPPOSITE: An ebony-stained bookcase serves as a console for the sofa and provides lots of room for books and display.

ABOVE: Pale gold paint with white trim wraps the room in subtle warmth, carrying the metallic gold tones of the wallcoverings to the rest of the space. I framed two of Michelle's African masks in simple white shadow boxes and showcased them at the foot of the stairs.

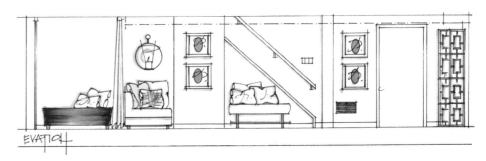

INDEX

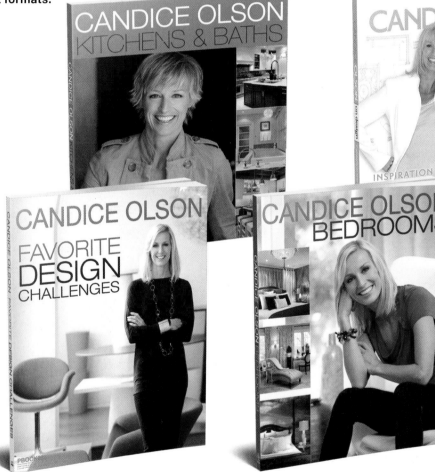
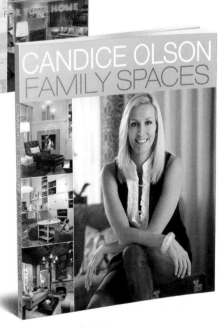